New Mexico Cooking

Southwestern Flavors of the Past and Present

by Clyde Casey

FISHER
BOOKS

Publishers: Bill Fisher
                         Helen Fisher
                         Howard Fisher
                         J. McCrary

Editor: Helen Fisher
Cover & Illustrations: David Fischer
Book Design: David Fischer
Book Production: Paula Peterson

Published by Fisher Books
4239 W. Ina Road
Tucson, AZ 85741
602-744-6110

Library of Congress
Cataloging-in-Publication Data

Clyde, Casey.
    New Mexico cooking : south-
    western flavors of the past and
    present / by Clyde Casey
         p.   cm.
    Includes index.
    ISBN 1-55561-059-5 : $12.95
    ($15.95 Can.)
    1. Cookery, American—South-
    western style. 2. Cookery—New
    Mexico.
I. Title.
TX715.2.S69C38   1994
641.59789—dc20
                            94-8949
                            CIP

CONTENTS

ABOUT THE AUTHOR

Clyde Casey is a multi-talented man—a well-known professional Western entertainer and songwriter, an award-winning sculptor and cook. He served as President of the Professional Artists of Colorado, and is a Western art historian, publishing *Western Art Beat* and *Beam Tab* for artists and collectors. Always seeking new interests to challenge his inquisitive mind, he is a resident of New Mexico.

DEDICATION

To my wife of over 40 years, without whom my life would have no meaning. Millie is my companion, my partner, and always my love.

INTRODUCTION

In 1960, while participating in a Barbershop Quartet show in Albuquerque, I was a guest for lunch at a restaurant in the Old Town Plaza. In the most pleasant of surroundings, I was served a trio of chile, beans, and corn dishes dressed with sauce and cheese. I was hooked. It was an instant love affair that has lasted for over 30 years. The clear assertive flavors and bright colors coupled with a sassy taste gave me an appetite and appreciation for this festive food, known throughout the world as New Mexico cuisine.

In this book I will share with you the most unusual and interesting of the dishes I have discovered over the years. Some are traditional recipes and others are contemporary, designed for our quick and convenient lifestyle. As you prepare these marvelous dishes you will learn that New Mexican food was special then and is just as special now. I hope you find, as I have, that once you experience the joy of this cooking, most other meals will seem bland and unexciting by comparison.

The bedrock of New Mexican cuisine is Native American, historically a simple, basic combination of chile, corn, beans, squash, wild fruits, nuts and game meat. This has been modified and augmented over the last 300 years to produce a truly unique cuisine. Today, the rich fusion of many culinary arts has created foods that are a blend of Spanish, Tex-Mex, Mexican, Pueblo Indian, French, Cowboy Chuckwagon, and Mediterranean influences. The surprising results of the melding of these traditional ethnic and imported specialties, that feature varieties and unusual combinations, are found nowhere else in the world. Each of the cultures who are a part of this state's rich, colorful history has contributed to this warm, savory cuisine.

The evolution of this cuisine was triggered with the arrival of the Spaniards in the early 1500s. They brought chickens, pigs, cattle, olives, grapes, rice, sugar, wheat, ground cinnamon and a variety of other spices. Later, in the mid-1800s, the French influence blended with the Spanish and Native cooking styles to create a rich, delicate, very diverse and yet distinctive style.

CHILE PEPPERS—The Fire in New Mexico Cooking

Chile peppers are the *fire* in New Mexico cooking. I will never forget the delightful smell of roasting chiles I encountered during my first trip to one of the many chile-pepper farms just outside Roswell, NM. Here the chile is considered a vegetable, not a spice. People dry strings of the brilliant red chiles, called *ristras,* and hang them outside their homes as decorations or as a sign of welcome. Some homes have a string of chiles hanging in the kitchen that are used for everyday cooking. They just pluck one off and grind it up as a food additive for everything from pizza to a topping for hors d'oeuvres. Also, the image of peppers is found on everything from Christmas decorations to men's underwear.

Today more chiles are grown and consumed than any other seasoning in the world. There is a common misconception that all chiles are hot; this is far from the truth. All chile peppers retain an element of unpredictability, but recent research indicates that peppers are important when it comes to burning calories. They also pick up taste, without adding any fat. We are just now beginning to fully understand the special role chiles play in New Mexico diet. They tingle your taste buds, not your nose.

There are hundreds of varieties of chiles; some even have similar names, which adds to the confusion. For example, *chile ancho* is dried *poblano.* The same chile in California is called *pasilla.* Other problems stem from differences in soil types and climatic conditions. All these variables go into creating a wide range of heat levels.

Capsaicin, known as 8-Methyl-N-vanillyl-6-noenamide, is the unwieldy chemical substance found in all chile peppers. This chemical gives the chile pepper its piquancy, which can range from innocent to outright incendiary. This oily, orange-colored acid is found in the seeds and veins of all chile pods. *New Mexico's No. 6,* formerly known as *anaheim chile,* has become popular across the country because of its relatively mild taste and appeal to those who have not yet become addicted to the hotter varieties.

The following heat scale guide was developed by Dr. Roy Nakayama of New Mexico University. This ranges from #1, lowest or coolest, to #10, the highest or hottest. Heat can be adjusted in any recipe by using the type of chile that best represents one's particular taste buds. While this guide is by no means exhaustive, it does represent the most frequently found commercially sold chiles.

10— Bahamian (Habanero)
 9— Santaca (Japanese)
 8— Tabasco or Serran   HOT
 7— Jalapeño
 6— Española and Cayenne (hotter)
 5— Sandia   MEDIUM
 4— Hot Ancho
 3— Numex Big Jim
 2— Rio Grande   MILD
 1— New Mexico No. 6, formerly known as Anaheim

New Mexico recipes often mix chiles, allowing one to enjoy the different taste sensations provided by each. Believe me, each type of chile does have its own distinctive taste. New Mexicans want the chile *flavor,* not just the *heat,* although many do seem to have a much higher threshold of pain than, say, New Englanders. Green or red, it is the chile *flavor* they crave. There are those who prefer the mature, slightly less hot red chile and those who want the green, immature, hotter version of the same chile.

Whenever possible, use fresh chile peppers. To maintain the best flavor the preparation of fresh chiles is important. When dealing with the hotter varieties, you cannot be faint of heart.

Chiles have an outer skin (Mother Nature's cellophane) which must be blistered and charred to separate it from the chile flesh. A barbeque grill, when used out-of-doors, is preferable when roasting chiles. Because it takes as long to char one chile as it does a dozen or so, you should prepare a batch. A bushel can be done in an hour or so. If you are only roasting a few, use your kitchen broiler.

Slit the chile with a small knife to allow the steam to escape during the roasting. Turn the chiles as needed, because the skin needs to blister. Try not to disturb the flesh underneath. After the chiles are charred evenly, remove them from the grill and place them in a heavy plastic bag. Seal the top with a twist tie and allow them to sit for at least 20 minutes. As they cool, the internal steam loosens the skin.

The more delicate varieties, such as *poblanos,* should be dipped in cold water when taken from the grill to stop the cooking action. Then peel them immediately. Over the years, during the chile harvest season, we have met a number of our new neighbors when they showed up, eyes watering, to find out what was causing the strange yet appealing smell coming from our barbeque grill.

Freshly gathered chiles peel quite easily and can be stored in a plastic bag in the refrigerator. They will stay fresh for two weeks. If you plan to freeze the chiles for later use—and they do freeze well—freeze them with the charred skin in place. If you plan to use the whole chile, slit along the side and carefully remove the inner white veins. A pair of small scissors works well. If you plan to purée, strip, or chop the chiles you should remove the stem, seeds, and veins.

A word of caution: It is always wise to take a few precautions when preparing chile peppers. The capsaicin oil, the stuff that makes them hot, is primarily located in the seeds and inner veins. Any contact with them can be dangerous. Therefore, use rubber gloves during the preparation to avoid spreading the irritating oil to the eyes, mouth and nose. Also protect your eyes from the vapors.

An alternate peeling method is to use hot oil to blister the skin. Heat the oil to 275F (135C), place chiles in hot oil for 1 minute or until the chiles are fully blistered. Remove from oil, cool and peel. They will not have the roasted flavor, but are preferred by some people.

Today, cooking with chiles is not only feasible, but it can be great fun. A number of farmers' markets and supermarkets throughout the United States offer both green and red fresh chiles. When purchased from your local market, they should be used or processed in 3 to 4 days. Dried and packaged chiles are becoming more common each year.

Chiles are an excellent source of vitamin A and C and also serve as a preservative in frozen or cooked-meat dishes. As the pods ripen, the carotene (vitamin A) and ascorbic acid (vitamin C) increase. Low in calories and high in potassium, chiles may speed up your metabolism and help you burn more calories, according to some studies. It is also thought that chiles may aid in treating asthma and allergies, and in preventing heart disease and cancer. Add to this the fact that new data shows they do not necessarily aggravate the stomach, medically speaking, and you soon realize why chile peppers are a hot item with cooks all across the country.

Many people confuse CHILI and CHILE. *Chili* spelled with an *"i"* is a mixture of spices along with one or more varieties of chile peppers and meat. Sometimes beans are added, but to a real connoisseur, chili is only the spices and meat, most often pork. *Chile* spelled with an *"e"* is simply the fruit of a particular plant. Because of its popularity, I have included a number of chili recipes and an additional collection of dishes that use chili as an ingredient. Wherever I have suggested one of my chili recipes, feel free to substitute your favorite chili, either homemade or canned. There is no question that one of New Mexico's major contributions to American cuisine is chili.

In 1976, a now-famous chili duel was fought between the late humorist, H. Allen Smith, author of many books and the article *Nobody Knows More About Chili Than I Do,* and Wick Fowler, creator of Four Alarm Chili Mix. Over a thousand spectators attended this cookoff held in the remote town of Terlingua, Texas. This was the start of a national phenomenon, the chili cookoff. Service clubs, national organizations and local groups use cookoffs as money-raising events. There are hundreds of cookoffs in cities across the country. It is estimated that three quarters of a million people attend these events each year.

"Chilimania" is not, as some might think, a masochistic desire to punish oneself, but rather an obvious sign of today's immigrants' contribution to a dynamic population mix. Many of these new Americans come from Mexico, Central America, the Caribbean, Asia or Africa, and they have one thing in common. For centuries their typically bland, inexpensive foods have been enhanced with chile peppers of one kind or another.

CORN—That Amazing Maize

Southwest cooks use corn in many forms. Hominy, a dried corn processed with lime in water, is used to make traditional dishes such as *Posole,* a favorite New Year's day good-luck dish. Cornmeal is made from the nutritional part of the corn kernel, the endosperm. It can be yellow, white or blue.

Corn was considered the essence of life to Native Americans. It had both religious and symbolic significance to these people, and is even considered to have a magical sacredness. In many tribal ceremonies corn meal is used as a prayer offering to the gods. Even today, when a Hopi girl decides to propose marriage to a boy, she makes a large plate of piki bread and leaves it on his doorstep. If the bread is taken into the house, he has accepted her proposal. Similarly, the Zunis scatter cornmeal in their prayer ceremonies to celebrate birth, death, sunrise and sunset. In contrast, Navajos believe that a giant turkey hen once flew across the sky and dropped an ear of blue corn from under her wing, and thus it became sacred.

According to archaeologists, corn was cultivated as early as

A.D. 217 by the Basket Maker culture of the Southwest. Amazingly, kernels of corn dating to approximately 3600 B.C. have been discovered in New Mexico's Bat Cave.

In New Mexico, we find two-dozen varieties of corn with colors ranging from white to blue and from yellow to bright red. Each of the colors has significance to the Indians. Sweet yellow is eaten roasted on the cob. To make flour, hominy, tamales and bread, white is used. The blue is frequently used for baking and drinks. Red was used for piki, a brittle bread, a predecessor of today's tortilla.

The tortilla is an American Indian invention. Corn is soaked in water that contains lime to make the skins come off. Then the softened kernels are ground into a smooth dough called *masa* and patted into thin round cakes. Cultivated corn, often processed with wood ash, provided the Indians with iron and improved amino-acid balance. Indians rarely suffered from pellagra, as did many on non-corn based diets. Corn is the primary ingredient of many nations' food chains and one of our most important cash crops. The United States produces over half the world's supply of this versatile, nutritious food.

Corn's simple carbohydrate structure was the primary leg of the Indian's food triad. Because it required little or no care after planting, Indians could plant it in an appropriate location, usually on the flat rich soil near a stream, and return only in the fall to harvest that which had survived the animals and Mother Nature's scourges. For thousands of years the Southwest Plains Indians were nomadic. And because the corn was self-sustaining they were free to roam, hunting for game, berries, and plants.

BEANS—Sustenance from a Pod

There are those who credit the lowly bean for the start of the villages and the cities that followed in the Southwest. Because beans required more care and tending, the planting of beans meant the end of the nomadic roaming of the Southwestern Indians. The bean added complex carbohydrates which balanced the simple carbohydrates of corn. This combination, which we now recognize as an ideal body fuel, is said to have been the energy of the plains. The protein that was found in the bean was critical to survival, as the increasing population of the Southwest made game scarce and harder to find. Squash added the third element, which was oil from the seeds. With corn, beans, squash seeds, piñon nuts, chiles, wild berries and plants, the Indians had the eight essential amino acids necessary for a well-balanced diet. Because beans were relatively easy to grow, they became increasingly important as the buffalo and other wild game disappeared from the harsh land of New Mexico.

No single food was as important to the development of the West as the bean. From chuckwagon cook to gold miner, homesteader to the railroad gandy dancer driving his metal spikes, this little round bundle of carbohydrates was critical. Beans, sustenance in a pod, were to a New Mexican what potatoes were to the Irish, rice to the Chinese, or pasta to an Italian. It was the staple—cornerstone, if you will—of his diet. With the addition of many different varieties to augment the little speckled brown pinto bean that improves every time you heat it, today beans are no less important to Southwest cuisine than they were 300 years ago.

It was common for the Indian farmers to plant corn and squash, and then add beans in the same row. As the corn reached a few inches high, the beans would use the corn stalk as a bean pole. The corn plant then shaded the squash. The squash leaves, an ideal ground cover, conserved any moisture that happened along.

In recent years, a "new" type of bean has made it to the supermarket shelves. It is called an *Anasazi* bean and it is quite expensive. White with large splotches of red, it looks rather weird and unappetizing, but it is sweeter than a pinto. But make no mistake about it, the pinto is still King here in the Land of Enchantment. This dappled dandy that cooks up pink is what the New Mexicans mean when they call for beans in a recipe.

There are many schools of thought when it comes to cooking beans. Some soak the beans overnight; others say there is no need to pre-soak them at all. Choose whatever method suits you best from the following three options:

If you do not plan to soak overnight, wash 2 cups of beans, remove debris or broken or bad beans, and add 8 cups of water. Remove any beans that float to the top. Add 2 tablespoons of bacon grease or lard and 2 cloves of garlic. Bring to a full boil in a large kettle and simmer for 3 or 4 hours adding hot (boiling) water as needed. Keep water level slightly higher than the top of the beans. Continue cooking until the beans are tender. Add 2 teaspoons of salt before serving.

For soaking the beans, wash 2 cups of beans and remove any

debris, broken or bad beans. Cover with cold water and remove any beans that float to the top and then let them sit overnight. Drain and rinse well. Place in a large kettle and add bacon grease or lard. Bring to a boil and cover. Simmer for 1-1/2 to 2 hours or until tender.

I prefer to use a pressure cooker. I use 2 cups of washed and sorted beans, and place them with 8 cups of water in a pressure cooker. Next I bring the water to a gentle boil for about 10 minutes and add the bacon grease. Then I remove them from the heat, put the lid on the cooker and let them sit for at least 2 hours. One hour before I intend to eat, I add 2 teaspoons of salt, cover and bring the cooker up to 15 lbs. of pressure for 12 minutes. Then I remove them from the stove and allow the pressure to drop naturally.

TORTILLAS—The Southwest Bread of Life

No other food product is as versatile as the tortilla. Corn or flour, this staple of most New Mexican cooking is its most important ingredient. With no refrigeration, the use of dry food during the winter months was critical to the Indian's survival. Corn, because it stores well and is quickly ground, was ideal. It was ground into masa, formed and shaped by hand into a flat, round, thin pancake. This was used as a food scoop and wrapper for a variety of recipes using peppers, corn, and beans.

Today, an endless variety of recipes—tacos, burritos, chimichangas, enchiladas, quesadillas, flautas, tostadas—all depend on these little thin cakes of corn or flour for their existence. With sauces, salsa, and toppings, they are the heart and soul of New Mexican cuisine.

There are many recipes for the construction of tortillas. Making tortillas is really an art form and takes years of practice to get it right. To watch somebody who truly knows the art is a real pleasure. Many times I have watched my brother's wife pat them out and make a nice, neat, flat cylindrical stack. Unfortunately, when I try it the stack looks more like a pile of flat innertubes. Fortunately, quality tortillas are available in almost every market that offers other bread products. I have included several excellent recipes for bread, cakes and other baked items not available at your local market.

Writing this book has been a pleasure. I have enjoyed every minute of it, and I will never forget the many wonderful people who willingly shared their unique knowledge and recipes with me. My culinary studies have taught me a great deal about the peerless people who call this beautiful land their home. It also has given me an added appreciation for the American Indians, whose home we now share.

The Appendix includes a partial list of those who shared their family recipes with me. If I have unwittingly forgotten anyone, I hope you forgive me. I would especially like to say thank you to Marge Sanchez, Nellie Fields, and Yolanda Martinez. Each is a cook of extraordinary talents. I have long since lost track of exactly what the source is of many of the recipes presented here as they have been given to me on scraps of paper, many verbally. One came anonymously in the mail from a woman whom I had met at a chili cookoff in Las Cruces.

I have included some simple, quick recipes as well as some that are very complex, requiring time and patience. Each has its place, because you will find, as I have, that the more you prepare this cuisine, the more you will want to be challenged.

It is my belief that there is no such thing as ownership of recipes—they are to be shared and enjoyed. Each one must stand on its own. I have done my best to present you with those I consider special in some way or another. I hope you find them as interesting and pleasing to your palate as I have. I personally know each to be worthy of your efforts.

So, what are you waiting for? Head for the kitchen and try them out. Meanwhile, from the Land of Enchantment—*mucho gusto!*

Clyde W. Casey
Roswell, New Mexico

GLOSSARY

ACHIOTE SEEDS are the dried reddish seeds of the annatto tree, used to give food a deep red color. Before they can be used, they are usually soaked overnight in water, and then ground into a paste. They impart a flavor that is earthy, subtle and hard to describe. They are sometimes available in brick form.

ANISE SEED is a small, elongated seed that tastes like licorice.

AVOCADO: A fruit with leathery skin and a soft, buttery flesh that yields to light pressure when ripe. A hard avocado will ripen if left at room temperature for two or three days. The Haas, or California type, is smaller and darker green than the emerald type grown in Florida, and some say it is more flavorful as well. Keep avocado flesh from discoloring by brushing it with lemon juice as it is peeled.

BEANS take time to prepare properly, but the result is a tender bean that is still firm. Canned beans are sometimes mushy, but they are convenient to keep on hand and the liquid in which they're canned adds flavor to many recipes. Dried beans keep almost indefinitely. Before cooking dried beans, rinse them well and pick them over for stones or inferior beans. The following types of beans are often used in Southwestern and New Mexican recipes:

Black beans *(frijoles negros, turtle beans)*: Though small, these beans have a hearty flavor. South American cooking makes great use of them. With their dramatic dark purple-blue color, they lend themselves nicely to garnishes.

Black-eyed peas *(cowpeas)*: The seeds of the cowpea, an annual vine. They are tan with a blackish spot, hence "black-eyed."

Garbanzo beans *(chick-peas)*: Spanish in origin, these rounded, beige beans have a nutty flavor.

Pinto beans *(frijoles)*: These charmingly brown-speckled beans have a pale or pinkish background.

CAYENNE: See Chile.

CHAYOTE *(christophine, mirliton, vegetable pear)*: Related to gourds, chayote squash have none of their brilliant decoration. Light-green skin encases firm flesh of an even paler green. Chayote may be baked, steamed, stuffed, or sautéed. A 1-lb. Chayote makes a nice serving for two or three people.

CHEESE: Traditional Mexican cheeses were made with goat's or sheep's milk. The following cheeses, all common to the Southwest, are used in this style of cooking:

Cheddar is a mild, firm cheese of English origin that becomes more sharp with age. It melts beautifully.

Chihuahua *(queso menonita)* is white, creamy and, like Muenster, sometimes is sold like string cheese. Mozzarella or Monterey Jack may be substituted.

Colby is a slightly sharp cheese with a flavor similar to that of Cheddar.

Monterey Jack is a mild cheese usually sold in blocks. It softens at room temperature.

Queso Añejo is an aged, hard grating cheese. It ranges from pale cream to white in color and is quite salty. Parmesan may be substituted.

Queso Fresco has a texture similar to farmer's cheese. A reasonable substitute for this crumbly cheese is Feta cheese.

Sierra is another rather dry sharp cheese that grates easily. Romano or Parmesan may be substituted.

CHILES are members of the pod-bearing capsicum family. New strains of chiles are developed frequently; there are hundreds of varieties. In their dry whole, crushed, or powdered form they are the heart and soul of New Mexico cuisine. Fresh, they have no match and are considered a vegetable, not just a spice. Do not confuse these with chili powder which generally consists of ground chile, cumin, salt, and garlic powder. To quench the fire of a too-hot mouthful of chiles, use milk, yogurt, sour cream, ice cream, or starches like bread or rice. Alcohol also dissolves the hot capsaicin which causes the burn. Fresh chile is seasonally available, but canned and dried are available year round. Here are some varieties you will encounter in New Mexican cooking:

Ancho refers to a ripened, dried poblano chile.

Cascabel chiles are difficult to find in their pure form in most parts of the United States. Sometimes dried anaheim chiles are labeled *cascabel,* but they are very different from the real item. Fresh cascabel chiles have a distinctive flavor and are hot. They are round and 1-1/2 inches in diameter. Dried, the cascabel chile has a nut-like flavor.

Cayenne chiles are pencil-thin and tapered, three to seven inches long. Dark green (unripe) or bright red (ripe), the cayenne is incendiary and well known to Cajun kitchens. The red ones are dried and ground to make cayenne pepper ("ground red pepper"). This product adds heat and just a little chile flavor.

Chipotle chiles are smoked, dried jalapeños with a very wrinkled appearance. Fresh jalapeños are vibrant green, but they turn brown when smoked. Chipotles can be purchased loose (dry) or canned in Adobo sauce. The canned variety is especially convenient, as it saves having to soak and soften them.

Habanero chiles are originally from Havana, and are said to be the hottest peppers in the world,

30 to 50 times hotter than a jalapeño. Closely related to the Scotch bonnet peppers of the Caribbean, they are lantern shaped, pungent and fruity, with an apricot-like aroma.

Jalapeño chiles are the most famous chiles in the world. They range from hot to very hot. They are dark green, and similar in shape to serranos, about three inches long with a characteristically rounded tip. Peppers with the sharpest tips are the hottest. Jalapeños ripen to red. They take their name from Jalapa, the capital of Veracruz, Mexico. They are sold fresh, pickled, or canned. When dried and smoked, they are called *chipotle peppers.*

New Mexican chiles are slim, ranging between five and eight inches long, and of various light shades of green. Also know as *anaheim chiles,* these mildly hot peppers are sometimes twisted in appearance. They are not normally stuffed because their flesh is thin and more fragile than that of the poblano chiles. The New Mexican cultivated extensively in New Mexico when ripe and red are sometimes know as *chiles colorados.* New Mexican chiles are dried and tied in strings (ristras), or ground and blended in commercial chili powder mixtures. They may be purchased in cans as "mild green chiles." These peppers were named after the town that, at the turn of the century, was the site of a chile-pepper cannery.

Pasilla chiles means "little raisin" in Spanish. This long, thin, dry, red-brown chile has a dusty raisin-like taste. They are hot and a little spicier than the ancho.

Poblano is the chile most frequently used for chile rellenos. It is a suave dark green and ranges from mild to hot. These chiles look like a deflated bell pepper; the poblano has a nice shape for stuffing.

Red Pepper Flakes are just that—flaked, dried ripe chiles. Most red pepper flake mixtures are quite hot.

Serrano chiles are a sort of middling green, developing to brilliant red when ripe. Extremely hot (as hot as any New Mexican chile), this chile is usually shorter and thinner than the jalapeño. It is the mainstay in salsas.

CHOCOLATE has been credited to the Aztecs. It was probably first used to flavor a bitter drink favored by their mystics. Another Mexican invention, the *molinillo*, is a wooden whisk used to whip

hot chocolate. The handle is rolled between the palms of the hands, whipping the mixture until it is frothy. Today, block Mexican chocolate frequently contains cinnamon, vanilla, clove and ground almonds.

CHORIZO is a spicy smoked pork (or pork and beef) sausage, available both in links and in bulk.

CILANTRO *(Mexican Parsley, Chinese Parsley, fresh Coriander)* is an herb which bears a resemblance to flat-leaf parsley, but the flavor is entirely different: strong, fresh, acid. Cilantro is perishable; store it in the refrigerator with the stems in water and plastic loosely covering the leafy tops.

CINNAMON is truly a spice of Mexican cuisine, used in dishes sweet and savory. It is available ground as a powder or in tightly rolled dry quills.

CORIANDER is the seed of the plant that gives us cilantro. It has a dusky flavor that is often associated with Eastern cooking. It may be purchased ground or as whole dried seeds.

CORN HUSKS are dried corn husks, softened by soaking, and are used to wrap food before it is cooked. They make a sort of natural jacket that holds a mixture together as it steams. Remove any silk clinging to the dried husk before using. Several small corn husks may be overlapped for a larger wrapping—as for a tamale.

CORNMEAL is, of course, the staple of Southwestern larders. When cornmeal is called for, use yellow or white, coarsely or finely ground. Blue cornmeal has become very popular and is now widely available.

CUMIN is a powerful, sometimes dominating spice so often used in traditional Southwest cooking. Recipes may call for whole cumin seed or for ground cumin.

EPAZOTE is a herb widely used in Mexican cooking, and is now becoming more popular in New Mexico. Usually available as dried, this herb is said to ease digestion.

FRIJOL is the Spanish word for *bean*. See Beans.

GROUND RED CHILES become pure chili powder when finely ground from dried red chiles. This is not blended chili powder.

GROUND RED PEPPER is made from ground dried cayenne chiles; this is often called *cayenne pepper*. See Chile, Cayenne.

GUAVA is a yellow-green fruit with pale, faintly pink flesh, about the size of a plum. It is intensely fragrant when ripe. Guava paste is only one of the fruit pastes beloved of Hispanics, often served with cream cheese as dessert. The fruit is cooked with sugar until thick, then canned or shaped into blocks.

HOMINY is yellow or white corn kernels that have been soaked in lime to remove their husks. Now available dried, frozen or canned, hominy is an important ingredient of many special recipes.

JÍCAMA is a bulky, brown-skinned root vegetable that looks like a sharp-tasting turnip, but is so mild in flavor that, when eaten raw, it is usually sprinkled with lemon or lime juice and chili powder. After the brown fibrous skin has been pared away, jícama flesh does not discolor. Look for smallish jícama, which will be sweet and moist.

JUNIPER BERRIES are the fruit of an evergreen, the berries that give gin its distinctive flavor. These blue-green berries are usually purchased dried. Use sparingly for a subtle flavor.

LARD has been, perhaps, the most frequently used ingredient in traditional New Mexican cooking. Fresh rendered lard is rarely available and the processed flavorless blocks in your supermarket are of little value. I have used vegetable oil in most recipes. If you have fresh lard available, by all means use it. There is no substitute for the taste it offers. It should be noted that lard, for all its reputation, has approximately half the cholesterol of butter.

MANGO, one of the most popular fruits in Mexico, is becoming more popular here in New Mexico. It has a peach-like taste and flowery aroma. The flesh is juicy and deep yellow. To slice the fruit, free it from the pit in large pieces.

MASA literally means "dough" in Spanish. Masa is cornmeal dough made from dried corn kernels that have been softened in a lime (calcium hydroxide) solution, then ground. Fresh frozen masa is sometimes available in your super market. Masa comes finely ground in a dehydrated form and can be used to make tortillas and tamales.

MOLE is the Spanish word for "mixture." There are dozens of mole sauces which use countless combinations of ingredients. Among them are meats, spices, vegetables and a multitude of flavorings. One of the most common ingredients of mole sauce is chocolate.

NOPALES are the leaves (pads) of the prickly pear (nopal) cactus. They are firm and crunchy. Let size be your guide in buying them; the smaller the pad, the more likely it is to be tender. Use tweezers to remove the spines, a sharp paring knife or vegetable peeler to remove their bases. With a flavor similar to green beans, nopales are eaten both raw and cooked.

NON-REACTIVE PAN: Certain metals, especially aluminum, react with the acids in chiles and tomatoes. They can actually leach the metal away. Non-reactive cookware is stainless steel, copper, glass, plastic or clay. Aluminum pans with a Teflon or other protective coating are considered non-reactive. Do not store processed chiles or tomatoes in aluminum containers.

NUTS: Important flavoring agents in Southwest cooking, nuts are sometimes ground and stirred into sauces as a thickening agent. In addition to giving the sauce more body, raw nuts add their own particular flavor. Toasted nuts are more often used as a garnish or in baking. Pecans, peanuts, and Pine (Piñon) are

popular nuts in New Mexico.

Toasting Nuts enhances their flavor. To toast nuts, spread them in a single layer in an ungreased pan; bake at 350F (175C), stirring and checking until they are done. Nuts are toasted when they are lightly browned. Bake almonds, pecans and walnuts 7 to 12 minutes. Pine nuts toast more rapidly, 5 to 7 minutes.

Ground Nuts are often required in Southwestern recipes. To grind nuts, place 1/3 to 1/2 cup at a time in the work bowl of a food processor or blender. Process them in short pulses just until ground (longer, and you will have nut butter).

PAPAYA is a nearly oval fruit with creamy golden yellow skin, orange yellow flesh and scores of shiny black seeds conveniently packed in its center. When slightly under-ripe, the flesh is firm (perfect for making into relishes); when ripe, it is soft and very juicy.

PECAN is an oil-rich native American nut. See Nuts for toasting and grinding.

PEPPER comes in many forms. There is PIPER NIGRUM (Peppercorn), CAPSICUM FRUTECENS and CASPSICUM ANNUUM, the family of vegetables known variously as *peppers* and *chiles.* Peppercorns came to the Western world originally from Madagascar. The success of medieval spice traders made black pepper more widely available and only a little less precious than it had previously been. BELL PEPPERS are related to chile peppers, but lack the capsaicin; bell peppers are, therefore known as "sweet." Until recently, bell peppers of any color other than green were rarely available. Today, there is a profusion of red, yellow and even purple. Red and yellow are the sweetest.

PILONCILLO is an unrefined sugar, that can be purchased in hard cones. Like other "raw" sugars, piloncillo is beige to brown. The deeper the color, the more pronounced the molasses flavor.

PINE NUTS *(Piñons, Pignolis)* are the seeds of the Piñon pine. They are delicious raw or toasted. Store them tightly covered and either refrigerated or frozen, depending on how quickly they are to be used. See NUTS for toasting and grinding.

PLANTAIN, a relative of the banana, boasts a thick skin and large size. The fruit itself tends to be a deeper yellow than that of the banana. Cooked, unripe plantain is eaten as one would a potato. Plantains are sweetest when ripe, which isn't until their skins are an alarming black. Like bananas, plantains will ripen after they have been harvested.

POSOLE is sometimes called hominy, but the word *posole* authentically refers to a dish made with hominy as an ingredient. See HOMINY.

PRICKLY PEAR is the diminutive (egg-size) fruit of the cactus of the same name. It is nearly impossible to avoid the prickles when peeling to reveal the garnet-colored flesh. Prickly pears are sometimes sold with the prickles removed.

PUMPKIN SEED, with the shells or husks removed, are known as *pepitas.* Store them in a cool, dry place. To toast pumpkin seeds, spread them in a single layer in an ungreased pan. Bake at 350F(175C) 13 to 15 minutes, stirring and checking frequently.

QUESO is the Spanish word for cheese.

RED PEPPER: See Ground Red Pepper.

RED PEPPER SAUCE, a commercially bottled condiment, is made from vinegar, spices and hot chiles. It adds heat, but little in the way of flavor.

RICE is a very important staple in Mexican cooking. Mexican cooking calls for long- or medium-grain white rice. An occasional Southwestern dish uses wild rice, which really isn't rice. It is the seed of an aquatic grass once harvested only by Native American who lived by the Great Lakes.

SQUASH BLOSSOMS, the blossoms used in Southwestern cooking, are (contrary to popular belief) those of winter squashes such as pumpkin, not zucchini. They are a perishable item and are best used the day they are bought.

TAMARIND is an intensely pungent, tart pod about four inches long. Tamarind is usually bought packaged in a tightly compressed, sticky plastic-wrapped lump. The flesh is riddled with fibers and seeds—not what you want in your food—and must be soaked before using. Separate the tamarind pods, pulling away and discarding as much of the outer skin as you can. Cover with water and let the pulp soak for at least an hour (overnight, if time permits). Then squeeze the pulp well to extract the juice or rub as much pulp as you can through a fine mesh sieve.

TEQUILA is a pale, sharp-tasting liquor distilled from the agave plant, which thrives in an arid, hot climate like the central plains of Northern Mexico. The stem of the agave, known also as the *century plant,* is used in making both pulque, a fermented, rather bitter beverage, and tequila.

TOMATILLO are fat little vegetables the size of robust cherry tomatoes. They grow in papery husks reminiscent of Japanese lanterns and taste best when they are brilliant green in color. By the time they begin to turn yellow, they have lost some of their acid freshness. This happens when they are lightly cooked too, but then, although they relinquish their vibrant color, they develop a gentler flavor and become more luscious. Uncooked, chopped tomatillos are the basis for chunky green salsas. Select tomatillos with their husks still drawn tightly around them. Husk and rinse off the sticky residue before using them.

TOMATO is a plant native to South America, widely cultivated for its edible, fleshy, usually red fruit. Roasting tomatoes gives them a faintly mysterious flavor. It works best with truly ripe, red tomatoes. To roast and peel tomatoes, set the oven control to broil. Arrange cored tomatoes with their top surfaces about 5 inches from the heat. Broil, turning occasionally, until the skin is blistered and evenly browned, about 5 to 8 minutes. The skins will be easy to remove. If the tomatoes are roasted on aluminum foil, the cleanup will be easy and you'll be able to save any juice they give off as they roast.

TORTILLA: Tortillas are round, flat unleavened breads made from ground wheat or corn. They are the basis of Mexican cookery. Tortillas are rolled, folded, used as dippers, fried crisp and munched fresh. Corn tortillas are cut into wedges and fried for chips. For the best chips, fry tortillas that are at least one day old. Flour tortillas, softer than those made from corn, are becoming more popular in New Mexico. Commercially made tortillas of both kinds are best stored in the freezer until needed. To soften tortillas, warm them on a hot ungreased skillet or griddle for about 30 seconds to 1 minute. They can be warmed in a 250F (120C) degree oven for 15 minutes. Or, wrap several in dampened microwaveable paper toweling or microwave plastic wrap and microwave on HIGH (100% Power) for 15 to 20 seconds.

TRIPE usually means the linings of pig and sheep stomachs. Tripe is the identifying ingredient of traditional MENUDO, a hearty soup. Tripe needs to be thoroughly rinsed in three or four changes of cold water before it can be used.

WALNUTS are a delicious complement when used with corn. See NUTS for toasting and grinding.

APPETIZERS

For many years the crisp nibble of a fresh tortilla chip dipped in sassy salsa has been the dominant appetizer of New Mexico. In the last few years *nachos,* tortilla pieces topped with melted cheese and sprinkled with jalapeño peppers, have become very popular. They are served everywhere—from cocktail lounges to sporting events. I have included a simple nacho recipe. You can add any number of toppings including refried beans, chopped green onions and black olives, which are very good.

For your next party, please try my Mexican Shrimp Cocktail. Make sure that you fix a large amount as this dish will be a hit. Jícama with Fresh Limes is another simple appetizer that adds contrasting texture and flavors. Your health-conscious guests will welcome it. If you add my Corn & Pecan Dip, make sure you have copies of the recipe ready for your guests. I've given away more copies than I can count since I first tasted this dip at an art show in Taos, years ago.

❧ AVOCADO DIP ❧

3   medium avocados
2   tablespoons lemon juice
1/2   teaspoon salt
1/4   teaspoon black pepper
1   cup dairy sour cream
1/2   cup mayonnaise
1   (1-1/4-oz.) pkg. Taco Seasoning Mix
1   (21-oz.) can bean dip, plain or jalapeño
1   cup chopped green onions
3   tomatoes, seeded, and chopped
1   (7-oz.) can chopped olives
2   cups (8-oz.) shredded, sharp Cheddar cheese
   Tortilla chips

1. In a medium-size bowl, peel, pit and mash avocados. Add lemon juice, salt and pepper.

2. In a separate bowl, combine dairy sour cream, mayonnaise and taco seasoning.

3. To assemble, spread bean dip on a large shallow platter.

4. Spoon avocado mixture over bean dip. Top with dairy sour cream and taco mixture.

5. Sprinkle with chopped onions, tomatoes, and olives.

6. Cover with shredded cheese. Serve with tortilla chips.

Makes about 8 servings.

Notes..
....
....
....

❧ BEAN & GARLIC DIP ❧

　　2　cups cooked or canned pinto beans, drained
　1/4　cup mayonnaise or salad dressing
　　1　garlic clove, finely chopped
1-1/2　teaspoons ground red chile peppers
　1/4　teaspoon salt
　　　Dash of black pepper

1. Combine all ingredients in a medium-size bowl.

2. Cover and refrigerate 1 hour.

3. Serve with tortilla chips.

Makes 2 cups.

Refried beans are a staple in Southwest cooking. Here is how easy they are to make: Remove beans from the juice they have been cooked in and mash them with a potato masher, leaving some unmashed. Cook them in a cast-iron skillet with some bacon grease, season with garlic, then salt and pepper to taste.

Notes...
....
....
....

❧ BELL PEPPER RAJAS ❧

1/2   green bell pepper, seeded
1/2   yellow bell pepper, seeded
1/2   red bell pepper, seeded
3/4   cup shredded Monterey Jack cheese
1/4   tablespoon crushed red pepper
  2   tablespoons chopped ripe olives

1. Cut bell peppers into 6 strips each, then cut crosswise in halves.

2. Arrange pepper strips in an ungreased 9-inch-square broiler-proof pan.

3. Sprinkle with cheese, red pepper and olives.

4. Set oven to broil and broil peppers about 3 to 4 inches from heat.

5. Broil until cheese melts or about 3 minutes.

Makes 6 servings.

El Morro National Monument is located 58 miles southeast of Gallup on NM 53. This 200-foot castle of white sandstone bears the most historic collection of graffiti in the United States.

Notes..
....
....
....

❧ CARAMELIZED CARNITAS ❧

1-1/2 lbs. boneless pork shoulder
   2 tablespoons packed brown sugar
   1 tablespoon tequila
   1 tablespoon molasses
 1/2 teaspoon salt
 1/4 teaspoon black pepper
   2 garlic cloves, finely chopped
 1/3 cup water
   1 green onion with top, sliced

1. Cut pork into 1-inch cubes. Place cubes in single layer in a 10-inch skillet.

2. Top with remaining ingredients, except for green onion.

3. Bring to a boil, then reduce heat.

4. Simmer uncovered, stirring occasionally, until water has evaporated and the pork is slightly caramelized, about 35 minutes.

5. Sprinkle with green onion and serve with wooden picks.

Makes 10 servings.

Notes ....
....
....
....

❧ CORN & PECAN DIP ❧

---

    2   (8-oz.) pkgs. cream cheese, softened
  1/4   cup lime juice
    1   tablespoon ground cumin
    1   tablespoon ground red chiles
  1/2   teaspoon salt
        Dash black pepper
  1/4   cup vegetable oil
    1   (16-oz.) can whole-kernel corn, drained
    1   cup chopped pecans
    1   small onion, diced

1. In a large bowl, combine all ingredients except corn, pecans, and onion. Beat until smooth with electric mixer on medium speed.

2. Stir in corn, pecans, and onion. Spoon into a serving bowl.

3. Serve with tortilla chips.

Makes 4 cups.

Vegetable oil has a higher smoking point and a less distinct flavor than olive oil. By combining the two, you can enhance the flavor of the vegetable oil and raise the smoking point of the olive oil. This combination oil is a nice addition to your cooking.

Notes...
....
....
....

COWBOY CAVIAR

1   (15-oz.) can black beans, rinsed, drained
1   (4-oz.) can ripe olives, drained, chopped
1/4 cup finely chopped onion
1   garlic clove, finely chopped
2   tablespoons vegetable oil
2   tablespoons lime juice
1/4 teaspoon salt
1/4 teaspoon crushed red pepper
1/4 teaspoon ground cumin
1/8 teaspoon black pepper
1   (8-oz.) pkg. cream cheese, softened
2   large hard-cooked eggs, peeled, chopped
1   green onion with top, sliced

1. In a medium-size bowl, mix all ingredients except cream cheese, eggs and green onion.

2. Cover and refrigerate at least 2 hours.

3. Spread cream cheese on a serving plate.

4. Spoon bean mixture evenly over the cream cheese.

5. Arrange chopped eggs on bean mixture in ring around the edge of plate.

6. Sprinkle with green onion.

Makes 10 servings.

Notes..
....
....
....

❖{ DOUBLE CHEESE WHEEL }❖

---

   1   lb. Chihuahua, Gouda or Monterey Jack cheese
   1   (3-oz.) pkg. cream cheese, softened
 1/4 cup chopped, marinated artichoke hearts, drained
 1/4 cup toasted pine nuts
1-1/2 teaspoons chopped fresh basil or 1/2 teaspoon crushed
       dried-leaf basil
      Crackers or tortilla chips

1. If using Chihuahua or Gouda, remove wax coating or rind from cheese.

2. Hollow out cheese wheel with spoon or knife, leaving a 1/2-inch-thick shell on the sides and bottom and set aside.

3. Finely chop removed cheese to measure one cup. Reserve remainder for other use.

4. Place chopped cheese, cream cheese, artichoke hearts, 3 tablespoons pine nuts, and basil in a food processor and process until well mixed.

5. Pack mixture in the cheese shell and sprinkle with the remaining pine nuts. Press lightly.

6. Cover and refrigerate until firm, about 3 hours.

7. Cut into thin wedges and serve with assorted crackers or chips.

Makes 20 servings.

Notes..
....
....
....

❧ FISH IN ESCABECHE ❧

1   lb. firm white fish fillets, Orange Roughy, Haddock,
        or Mackerel, cut into 1/2-inch squares
1/3 cup lemon juice
1/3 cup lime juice
1/4 cup olive or vegetable oil
1   tablespoon fresh cilantro or 1 teaspoon dried-leaf cilantro
1   teaspoon oregano, fresh or 1/4 teaspoon dried-leaf oregano
3/4 tablespoon salt
1/4 teaspoon black pepper
12   pimiento-stuffed green olives
2   jalapeño chiles, seeded, chopped
1   small onion, finely chopped
1   garlic clove, finely chopped
1   cup tomato, seeded, chopped
1   avocado, peeled, chopped
     Saltine crackers or tortilla chips

1. Pour 3/4-inch water in a 10-inch skillet. Over medium heat, bring water to boil; carefully place fish in water. Heat to boiling; reduce heat.

2. Simmer uncovered until fish is opaque, about 30 seconds. Do not overcook or fish will fall apart. Drain carefully.

3. Mix remaining ingredients, except tomato and avocado, in a glass or plastic bowl. Stir in fish carefully.

4. Cover and refrigerate 2 days, stirring occasionally. Before serving, drain and gently stir in tomato and avocado.

5. Serve fish mixture on saltine crackers or tortilla chips.

Makes 6 servings.

Notes..
....
....
....

❧ JÍCAMA WITH ❧ FRESH LIMES

---

1   medium-small jícama
4   limes
1/2 teaspoon chile powder, cayenne pepper or paprika
    Salt

1. Using sharp knife, remove thick outer brown peel of jícama.

2. Rinse in cold water and cut into matchstick pieces.

3. Arrange jícama on a serving platter and squeeze the lime juice over them.

4. Sprinkle with chile powder, cayenne pepper or paprika. Use salt as a dip, if desired.

Makes 4 servings.

In 1821, the Santa Fe Trail was opened by the arrival of Captain William Becknell of Missouri as he led a small string of pack animals into Santa Fe Plaza. Wagon trains began to roll in with trade goods shortly thereafter. General Stephen Kearney marched into Las Vegas Plaza in 1846 and claimed the New Mexico Territory from Mexico for the United States of America.

Notes...
....
....
....

⋇{ MEXICAN SHRIMP }⋇ COCKTAIL

1	cup water
1/3	cup lime juice
1	garlic clove, finely chopped
2	teaspoons salt
	Dash of black pepper
24	raw shrimp, peeled, deveined
1	avocado, peeled, chopped
2	jalapeño chiles, seeded, chopped
1/4	cup chopped tomato
2	tablespoons chopped onion
2	tablespoons finely chopped carrot
2	tablespoons snipped, fresh cilantro
2	tablespoons vegetable oil
1-1/2	cups shredded lettuce
	Lemon or lime wedges

1. In a 4-quart dutch oven or heavy pot, heat water, lime juice, garlic, salt and pepper to boiling and reduce heat.

2. Simmer uncovered, until reduced to 2/3 cup.

3. Add shrimp. Cover and simmer 3 minutes. DO NOT OVERCOOK.

4. Immediately remove shrimp from liquid with slotted spoon and place in bowl of ice water. When cooled, drain shrimp.

5. Simmer liquid until reduced to 2 tablespoons and cool.

6. Mix reduced liquid, shrimp and remaining ingredients except shredded lettuce and lemon or lime wedges in glass or plastic bowl. Cover and refrigerate at least 1 hour.

7. Before serving, place lettuce on serving dishes. Top with shrimp and garnish with lemon/ lime wedges.

Makes 6 servings.

Notes...
....
....
....

❧ NACHOS ❧

Tortilla chips
1-1/2 cups (6 oz.) Cheddar cheese
6 jalapeño chiles, seeded, cut into slices

1. Place tortilla chips on 4 small ovenproof dishes or a pie pan.

2. Sprinkle each with 1/4 of the cheese and 1/4 of jalapeño slices.

3. Set oven to broil.

4. Broil about 3 to 4 inches from the heat until the cheese is melted. Serve at once.

Makes 4 servings.

These are a perfect microwave food. You can also garnish them with lettuce, tomatoes, black olives, onions or almost any raw vegetable. However, we do not recommend using Brussels sprouts. Sprinkle your chosen garnish in and around the chips. Experiment with a variety of combinations.

Notes...
....
....
....

❧ CHICKEN-CHILI PÂTÉ ❧

1/4	lb. chicken livers
1	tablespoon cooking oil
1-1/2	tablespoons butter
1	garlic clove, crushed
1	tablespoon onion, minced
3	cups peeled, finely chopped tomatoes
1	tablespoon chicken bouillon granules
1/4	teaspoon meat tenderizer, optional
1/4	teaspoon sugar
1/2	teaspoon salt
1/8	teaspoon black pepper
1/2	pkg. (8-oz.) cream cheese, softened
1/4	cup mayonnaise
1-1/2	tablespoons chopped, roasted, peeled, seeded green chiles
1/4	teaspoon horseradish
1	tablespoon dried parsley flakes

1. Preheat oven to 375F(190C). Pat chicken livers dry. Heat oil in a small skillet, fry livers until brown and fully cooked. Cool and chop finely.

2. In a saucepan, heat butter; sauté garlic and onion until limp. Add tomatoes, chicken bouillon, meat tenderizer, sugar, salt, and pepper. Cook until soft and mushy.

3. Remove from heat and cool. Add livers and stir well.

4. In a bowl, blend softened cream cheese with mayonnaise. Add chiles, horseradish, and mix thoroughly. Stir in parsley flakes.

5. Combine cheese and liver mixtures, pour into a shallow, 1-quart casserole. Bake uncovered 15 minutes or until slightly browned. Remove from oven and cool. Use as filling for Cornmeal Puffs, opposite.

Makes filling for 10 puffs.

Notes...
....
....
....

⋟{ CORNMEAL PUFFS }⋞

1/2   cup water
1/4   cup butter
1/4   teaspoon salt
1/2   teaspoon baking powder
1/2   cup sifted all-purpose flour
  2   tablespoons cornmeal
  2   large eggs
     Paprika

1. Preheat oven to 400F(205C). Grease cookie sheets.

2. In a saucepan, bring water to boil and add butter. Stir until melted.

3. Add dry ingredients and stir vigorously. Cook until the mixture draws away from sides of pan as you stir.

4. Remove from heat; cool 1 minute; add unbeaten eggs, one at a time, beating well after each addition until batter is smooth.

5. Drop batter by 1/2 teaspoons on prepared cookie sheets, 1-1/2 inches apart. Sprinkle each very lightly with paprika. Bake 15 minutes or until golden brown.

6. Allow puffs to cool completely. Gently slice off the top half of each puff, fill with cooled Chicken-Chili Pâté, opposite, and replace top.

7. Refrigerate 1 to 5 hours before serving.

Makes 10.

Notes...
....
....
....

SALADS & SOUPS

Robust salads and soups that can double as an entrée are very popular here. Years ago, in Questa, New Mexico I was introduced to Black Bean Salad. In my version of this recipe, I've added corn, which makes it very interesting with just the right amount of zest. I confess to using New Mexico chile peppers rather than bell peppers to pep up my own version.

Hearty soups remain popular here, Green Chile Potato Soup in particular. Of course we enjoy New Mexican Bean Soup year-round. Posole, a hearty hominy-based soup, is a must for the holiday season. In some homes the tradition is to serve it Christmas Eve, in others it's New Year's Eve. But whenever the weather is chilly, this warming soup is ideal fare.

Each household adopts their own version—one friend omits the ham hocks and substitutes chicken.

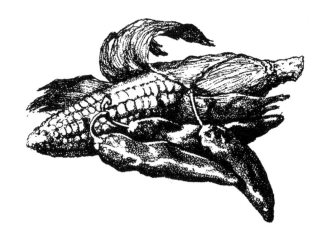

❧ BLACK-BEAN & ❧ CORN SALAD

2   cups cooked or canned black beans, drained
2   cups cooked or canned kidney beans, drained
2   cups cooked corn kernels
1   green bell pepper, diced
2   green onions, chopped
2   tablespoons vegetable oil
3   tablespoons red-wine vinegar
1   tablespoon honey
1/4 tablespoon dry mustard
1/4 teaspoon ground cumin
    Black pepper, to taste

1. In a large serving bowl, combine beans, corn, green pepper and green onions.

2. In a small jar, stir together oil, vinegar, honey, mustard, cumin and black pepper, to taste. Pour over the bean mixture, stir to coat all ingredients.

3. Cover and refrigerate until thoroughly chilled before serving.

Makes 6 servings.

Notes...
....
....
....

⊰ MEXICAN BEEF SALAD ⊱

3/4 lb. top round steak
1/2 teaspoon meat tenderizer
  3 tablespoons vegetable oil
  3 tablespoons vinegar
1/2 teaspoon salt
1/4 teaspoon ground cumin
1/4 teaspoon dried-leaf oregano, crushed
1/8 teaspoon garlic powder
1/8 teaspoon ground red pepper
  1 (16-oz.) can hominy, drained
  1 small onion, sliced
  1 green bell pepper, cut in rings
1/3 cup ripe olives
     Lettuce leaves
  4 cups torn lettuce
1/2 cup cherry tomatoes, halved
1/2 cup shredded Monterey Jack cheese

1. Partially freeze meat. Slice meat across grain into bite-size strips. Sprinkle with tenderizer.

2. In a 1-1/2-quart microwavable casserole, combine meat and 1 tablespoon oil. Cover with waxed paper. Cook in microwave on HIGH (100%) 3 to 5 minutes or until meat is done, stirring every 2 minutes.

Notes..
....
....
....

3. Remove meat, reserving drippings in casserole.

4. Add remaining oil to drippings, stir in vinegar, salt, cumin, oregano, garlic powder, and red pepper.

5. In microwave, cook uncovered on HIGH (100%) about 30 seconds or until bubbly. Add meat, hominy, onion, green pepper and olives. Toss gently to coat.

6. Line 4 salad plates with whole lettuce leaves. In large mixing bowl, combine meat mixture, torn lettuce and cherry tomatoes. Spoon mixture onto prepared plates; sprinkle with cheese.

Makes 4 servings.

Notes...
....
....
....

⊰{ TACO SALAD }⊱

---

 1   lb. lean ground beef
 1   garlic clove, minced
 1   (4-oz.) can chopped green chiles
1-1/2 cups chopped fresh tomatoes or 1 (16-oz.) can
       whole tomatoes
     Salt and black pepper, to taste
 1   cup dairy sour cream
 2   tablespoons lemon juice
1/4 teaspoon ground cumin
 6   corn tortillas
     Oil for frying
     Salt, to taste
 1   head lettuce, torn into bite-size pieces
 1   cup (4-oz.) grated Cheddar cheese
1/2 cup chopped green onions, including tops
 1   avocado, peeled, sliced

1. In a skillet, brown meat and garlic, stirring to break up meat.

2. Drain meat on paper towels and return to skillet.

3. Add chiles and tomatoes, with juices if using canned. Add salt and pepper to taste.

4. Cook over low heat 30 minutes, adding a little water if necessary. Mixture should have no liquid when fully cooked.

5. While meat cooks, prepare dressing. In a small bowl, combine dairy sour cream, lemon juice and cumin. Set aside.

Notes..
....
....
....

6. Cut tortillas in half, stack halves and cut in 1/2-inch strips. Heat about 1-inch oil in a skillet. Fry tortillas until crisp; drain on paper towels and sprinkle with salt to taste.

7. Before serving, arrange lettuce, cheese, tortilla strips, and onions in salad bowl.

8. Add meat mixture and toss lightly. Top with dressing and slices of avocado.

Makes 8 servings.

Notes..
....
....
....

❧{ GREEN-CHILE }❧ POTATO SOUP

---

  3   tablespoons butter
  8   green onions, chopped
  2   tablespoons all-purpose flour
  4   cups milk, heated
1/3 cup chopped, roasted, peeled, seeded green chiles
  3   medium potatoes, peeled, diced
      Salt to taste
  1   jalapeño or serrano pepper, seeded, minced
  1   cup grated Monterey Jack cheese

1. In a soup pot, heat butter and sauté onions.

2. When onions are soft, stir in flour, slowly stir in heated milk. Stir constantly until mixture begins to bubble.

3. Reduce heat to low and add chiles and potatoes; salt to taste.

4. Simmer 10 minutes or until potatoes are tender.

5. Scoop out 1 cup and purée in a blender or food processor.

6. Add purée back to pot and add jalapeño or serrano pepper. Cook 5 minutes more.

7. Serve with cheese sprinkled on top.

Makes 4 servings.

Notes..
....
....
....

NEW MEXICAN BEAN SOUP

3 cups dried pinto beans
2 quarts water
1 cup cubed salt pork
3 garlic cloves, chopped
1/2 onion, chopped
2 cups fresh cilantro, minced
3 roasted, peeled, seeded, chopped green chile peppers
4 cups whole canned tomatoes
Salt and black pepper

1. Rinse and sort beans, remove any debris and broken beans.

2. In a large pot, heat water. Add beans, salt pork and garlic. Cover and simmer 2 hours.

3. Add onion, cilantro, chile peppers and tomatoes. Cover and simmer 2 hours, or until beans are tender. Season to taste with salt and black pepper.

Makes 8 servings.

Notes..
....
....
....

❧ POSOLE ❧

---

4   (8-oz.) cans hominy
1   lb. fresh ham hock
1   lb. spare ribs
1   onion, chopped
1   garlic clove, minced
1   teaspoon dried-leaf oregano
1/4 teaspoon ground cumin
3   New Mexican green chiles, roasted, peeled, seeded,
       chopped
     Salt and black pepper, to taste

1. Rinse and drain hominy and place in a large pot; cover with cold water. Boil 1 hour, adding boiling water as necessary.

2. In another large pot, place ham and spare ribs. Cover with cold water. Bring to full boil. Remove from heat. Drain and rinse with cold water, drain again.

3. Add meat to hominy. Add onion, garlic, and oregano.

4. Cook over medium heat about 4 hours or until meat is tender.

5. Add chiles, salt and pepper to taste. Simmer for additional 30 minutes.

Makes 6 servings.

> *Some like to garnish with chopped fresh cilantro, sliced radishes, chopped green onions or a slice of avocado.*

Notes..
....
....
....

❧{ TWO-PEPPER SOUP }❧

3   green bell peppers
3   green chiles, roasted, peeled, seeded
1   small onion, chopped
4   cups chicken broth
2   tablespoons butter
2   tablespoons all-purpose flour
1   cup cream or evaporated milk
    Salt and black pepper, to taste
    Dairy sour cream

1. Rinse bell peppers and cut off stems. Place in a large pan of boiling water. Cover and cook about 5 minutes. Drain, peel, remove seeds and veins, and cut into quarters.

2. Pureé all peppers and onion in food processor or blender with 1 cup chicken broth.

3. In a large saucepan, melt butter; blend in flour, gradually stir in chile mixture and remaining chicken broth. Bring to a boil; reduce heat and simmer gently, constantly stirring, until soup is smooth. Blend in cream or undiluted evaporated milk. Heat through, but DO NOT BOIL. Season with salt and pepper to taste. Serve topped with dairy sour cream.

Makes 6 servings.

Notes..
....
....
....

BREADS

Corn tortillas are served as bread in almost all New Mexican homes. Each year flour tortillas become more popular, but it is doubtful that flour tortillas will ever replace corn. Because tortillas are so readily available, I have not included any recipes for them. I have selected some specialty breads for your enjoyment.

I would like to call your attention to the Navajo Fry Bread. This bread is very simple, served deliciously hot with honey or powdered sugar. I have watched Indian women make and fry these breads at pow wows and arts and crafts shows. I'm always amazed at how easily they take a ball of bread dough and, with a few quick patting motions, create a round flat shape ready for frying. They are a welcome addition to any meal.

Be sure to try the Jalapeño Corn Muffins, courtesy of Chef Jeff Pufal of the Pecos River Learning Center. You have never tasted any other muffins like these. Blue corn is an ingredient that we've enjoyed in New Mexico. It's gaining in popularity across the country as distribution improves. My Blue Corn Maple Muffins are a nice introduction to its unique flavor.

❧{ JALAPEÑO CORN }❧ MUFFINS

- 2   tablespoons shortening
- 1/4 cup butter, softened
- 1/4 cup sugar
- 2   large eggs
- 1/4 cup buttermilk
- 2   tablespoons minced jalapeño peppers
- 1/2 cup kernel corn
- 1/2 cup grated Monterey Jack cheese
- 1/2 cup grated Cheddar cheese
- 1/2 cup all-purpose flour
- 1/2 cup yellow or white cornmeal
- 1   teaspoon baking powder
- 1/2 teaspoon salt

1. Preheat oven to 375F(190C). Generously grease a muffin pan.

2. In a medium-size bowl, cream shortening, butter and sugar until smooth.

3. In a separate bowl, whisk the eggs and buttermilk together.

4. Slowly add the egg and milk mixture to the creamed butter mixture; continue to mix until combined well.

5. Add the jalapeño pepper, corn and cheeses; mix well.

6. In a separate bowl, combine the flour, cornmeal, baking powder, and salt.

7. Slowly add the dry ingredients to the wet ingredients and blend together well.

8. Pour into prepared muffin pans, filling three-quarters full. Bake in preheated oven about 18 minutes.

9. Serve warm with butter.

Makes 10-12 muffins.

Notes...
....
....
....

⊰ APPLE CRUNCH MUFFINS ⊱

1-1/2 cups unbleached flour, sifted
1/2 cup sugar
2 teaspoons baking powder
1/2 teaspoon salt
1-1/2 teaspoons ground cinnamon
1/4 cup vegetable shortening
1 large egg, slightly beaten
1/2 cup milk
1 cup cored, unpeeled, grated, tart apples
Nut Crunch Topping, recipe below

1. Preheat oven to 375F(190C). Place paper liners in muffin-pan cups.

2. Sift together flour, sugar, baking powder, salt and ground cinnamon into a medium-size bowl. Cut in shortening with pastry blender until fine crumbs form.

3. Combine egg and milk. Add to dry ingredients all at once, stirring just enough to moisten. Stir in apples.

4. Spoon batter into prepared muffin-pan cups, filling two thirds full. Sprinkle with Nut Crunch Topping.

5. Bake in preheated oven 25 minutes or until golden brown.

6. Serve hot with butter and homemade jelly or jam.

Makes 12 muffins.

NUT CRUNCH TOPPING
1-1/4 cup cups packed brown sugar
1/4 cup chopped pecans
1/2 teaspoon ground cinnamon

In a small bowl, mix together brown sugar, chopped pecans and ground cinnamon.

Notes..
....
....
....

❧ BLUE CORN MAPLE ❧ MUFFINS

1/4	cup melted butter or margarine
1/3	cup maple syrup
1	cup milk
1	egg, beaten
1	cup roasted blue cornmeal
1	cup unbleached flour
3	teaspoons baking powder
1/4	teaspoon salt

1. Preheat oven to 425 F(220C). Generously grease a muffin pan.

2. Combine melted butter or margarine with maple syrup and milk in a small bowl.

3. Beat in egg until smooth. In a separate bowl, stir together cornmeal, flour, baking powder, and salt.

4. Gently combine liquid ingredients with dry ingredients.

5. Spoon batter into prepared muffin-pan cups, filling three-quarters full.

6. Bake about 15 to 20 minutes or until lightly browned.

Makes 12 muffins.

Notes...
....
....
....

⊰{ BLUE CORNBREAD }⊱

1-1/2 cups blue cornmeal, or yellow or white cornmeal
   3 tablespoons sugar
   2 teaspoons baking powder
 3/4 cup milk
   1 egg, beaten
   3 tablespoons melted bacon fat, or oil
 1/4 cup crumbled cooked bacon
   1 (4-oz.) can chopped green chiles

1. Preheat oven to 350F(175C). Generously grease an 8-inch-square pan.

2. In small bowl, combine cornmeal, sugar and baking powder.

3. In another small bowl, mix the remaining ingredients. Combine the ingredients of both bowls and mix. Mixture should be moist.

4. Pour into prepared pan and bake 30 minutes, or until done.

5. Serve with Cinnamon-Honey Butter, page 157.

Makes 6 servings.

Notes...
....
....
....

✥ MEXICAN CORNBREAD ✥

- 1 cup yellow cornmeal
- 1 tablespoon baking powder
- 1 cup cream-style corn
- 1 onion, diced
- 1 cup dairy sour cream
- 1/2 teaspoon salt
- 2/3 cup melted butter
- 2 eggs, lightly beaten
- 1/4 cup grated Cheddar cheese
- 3 jalapeño peppers, seeded, deveined, diced

1. Preheat oven to 350F(175C). Generously grease a 9-inch-square baking dish.

2. In a medium-size bowl, combine cornmeal and baking powder and mix well.

3. Add corn, onion, dairy sour cream, salt, melted butter, eggs, cheese, and jalapeño peppers.

4. Stir well until blended. Pour into prepared baking dish and bake 1 hour.

Makes 10 servings.

> *Science News reported in 1988 that a single drop of capsaicin diluted in 100,000 parts of water will produce a persistent burning of the tongue. Diluted in one-million drops of water, it still produces a perceptible warmth.*

Notes..
....
....
....

❧ ROSWELL SPOONBREAD ❧

3-1/4 cups milk
   1 cup yellow cornmeal
  1/4 cup butter or margarine, melted
   1 teaspoon salt
   1 teaspoon sugar
   4 eggs, separated
  1/4 cup minced onion
   1 (4-oz.) can chopped green chiles

1. Preheat oven to 325F(160C). Generously grease a 2-quart baking dish. Heat milk in a double boiler over hot water. Gradually add cornmeal, stirring constantly. Cook until thick and mushy.

2. Remove from heat and stir in the butter, salt and sugar.

3. Beat egg whites until stiff and set aside.

4. In a large bowl, beat egg yolks until thick. Slowly mix in cornmeal mixture, then onion and chiles.

5. Fold in beaten egg whites.

6. Spoon into prepared baking dish, set dish in pan of hot water, and bake at 325F(160C), about 1 hour or until firm.

Makes 6 servings.

Notes..
....
....
....

⋖{ NAVAJO FRY BREAD }⋗

---

  2   cups all-purpose flour
  2   teaspoons baking powder
  1   teaspoon salt
  2   tablespoons shortening
2/3   cup lukewarm water
      Vegetable oil for frying
      Jam, honey or powdered sugar

1. In a medium-size bowl, combine flour, baking powder, and salt; cut in shortening until mixture has the appearance of fine crumbs. Sprinkle in water, 1 tablespoon at a time. Use a fork to toss until the flour is moistened and dough almost cleans side of bowl.

2. Dough should be soft, but not sticky. On a lightly floured surface, knead until smooth. Form into ball, cover, and refrigerate 30 minutes.

3. Heat oil in a large skillet to 400F(205C.) Tear off a piece of dough about the size of a peach. Pat and stretch until thin and round, about 6 to 8 inches in diameter.

4. Poke a hole through the middle, and drop into sizzling vegetable shortening.

5. Fry circles, turning once, until golden brown, about 1 minute on each side. Bread will puff beautifully.

6. Serve with jam, honey, or powdered sugar.

Makes 4 servings.

> *In New Mexico at fairs, craft shows, and Indian Pow Wows, you'll see long lines of people waiting to get their hot fry bread. Folklore tells us that poking a hole in the center lets out the evil spirits.*

Notes..
....
....
....

❧ ZUCCHINI NUT BREAD ❧

---

3   eggs
2   cups sugar
3   teaspoons vanilla extract
1   cup safflower or vegetable oil
2   cups grated unpeeled zucchini
2   cups all-purpose flour
1   cup whole wheat flour
1/4 teaspoon baking powder
1   teaspoon baking soda
2   teaspoons ground cinnamon
1/2 teaspoon grated nutmeg
1   cup chopped pecans

1. Preheat oven to 350F(175C). Generously grease and flour two 9 x 5-inch loaf pans.

2. In a large bowl, beat eggs until light and foamy; gradually beat in sugar. Continue beating and add vanilla extract and oil. Stir in grated zucchini. Sift in dry ingredients and fold in gently. Fold in pecans.

3. Divide mixture between prepared pans. Bake 1 to 1-1/4 hours. Cool on wire racks.

Makes 2 loaves.

Notes...
....
....
....

MAIN DISHES

Here I offer many old favorites, hand-picked to give you a true taste of this area. Whenever we have guests, they always ask if I'm going to fix Chicken Fajitas. This recipe can establish your reputation as a great cook. Because your guests assemble their own fajitas from the side dishes, they will suit their own taste and give you credit. A definite win-win situation. *Fajita* in Spanish means "little belts" as the strips of beef or chicken seem to resemble.

Chile Rellenos are a special dinner that present the chile as a vegetable entrée. Stuffed with cheese, batter-coated and quickly deep-fried, here is the chile pepper at its best. When you use fresh green chiles, there is no taste to compare with this dish. Even using frozen or canned chile you'll enjoy this great recipe.

Although I've no proof, I think Chicken-Fried Steak was invented in New Mexico. Perhaps it is the quality of beef we raise or the years of experience serving it, but whatever the case, we do it right. Follow my formula for a melt-in-your mouth dish that is guaranteed to impress any guest.

❧ BAKED-YAM FLAUTAS ❧ WITH PIÑON NUTS & SESAME SEEDS

- 2 lbs. yams, or winter squash (Acorn, Banana or Hubbard), seeded, halved
- 6 tablespoons butter
- 1 teaspoon sugar
- 6 flour tortillas
- 1/2 cup piñon nuts
- 2 tablespoons sesame seeds
- 1 tablespoon confectioners' sugar
- 1 cup dairy sour cream

1. Heat oven to 375F(190C). Place yams or squash pieces in oven and bake 1 to 1-1/4 hours, until yams or squash are soft in the center.

2. Remove pulp from yams or squash and place in bowl, add 2 tablespoons of butter and 1 teaspoon sugar. Stir with fork.

3. Place about 1/3 cup yam filling in center of each tortilla.

4. Roll up tortilla, folding ends in, sealing filling. Fold like an envelope—fold one edge to center, then fold over right and left end and roll. Secure with woodenpick. Set aside.

5. In an ungreased skillet, combine piñon nuts and sesame seeds. Toast, stirring over medium heat 2 to 3 minutes, until browned.

6. In a large frying pan, over medium heat, melt 2 tablespoons of butter until foaming. Add 3 or 4 flautas and fry 1 minute. Turn over and

Notes..
....
....
....

fry until brown and crisp, about 1 minute.

7. Remove to a warm platter. Add remaining butter and continue frying until all flautas are cooked.

8. Stir confectioners' sugar into dairy sour cream. Top each flauta with the sweetened dairy sour cream. Sprinkle roasted piñon nuts and sesame seeds on top. Serve warm and crunchy.

Makes 6 servings.

Notes..
....
....
....

⊰{ BLUE-CORN ENCHILADAS }⊱

1/3   cup oil
12   blue or yellow corn tortillas
3   cups Basic Red Sauce, page 129
3   cups grated Longhorn cheese
2   small onions, minced
4   eggs

1. Preheat oven to 275F(135C). Heat oil in a skillet.

2. Fry tortillas in oil until soft; drain on paper towels.

3. In a medium-size saucepan, heat chile sauce. Layer three tortillas on an ovenproof serving plate or shallow casserole, top each with grated cheese, Basic Red Sauce, and minced onions.

4. Place in preheated oven to melt cheese.

5. Fry eggs in remaining oil.

6. Top each enchilada stack with fried egg. Serve immediately.

Makes 4 servings.

Notes...
....
....
....

✧{ GREEN CHILE }✧ ENCHILADAS

---

 3 large green chiles, roasted, peeled, seeded, deveined
 1 tablespoon oil
 1 to 1-1/2 lbs. lean ground beef
   Salt and fresh ground black pepper, to taste
   Water
12 tortillas
   Oil for frying
 2 cups grated Cheddar or Monterey Jack cheese
 1 chopped onion
12 corn tortillas

1. Cut chiles into thumb-size pieces. Set aside.

2. In a skillet, heat 1 tablespoon oil. Season meat with salt and fresh ground pepper. Brown meat in oil.

3. Stir in chiles and cover with water. Cook 20 minutes.

4. Preheat oven to 250F(120C).

5. In a skillet, heat oil. Fry tortillas in a small amount of oil until they are firm. Remove from oil; dip into chile mixture, covering entire surface; remove and place on an ovenproof plate or shallow casserole and top with a spoonful of cheese and onion. Continue until all tortillas are stacked 3 high on each plate. Spoon remaining chile-meat mixture over each stack; sprinkle with cheese and bake in preheated oven 20 minutes. Serve at once.

Makes 4 servings.

Notes...
....
....
....

❧ ENCHILADAS VERDES ❧

---

    2   whole chicken breasts
    1   cup chicken broth
    2   (3-oz.) pkgs. cream cheese
    2   cups heavy cream
  3/4   cup finely chopped onions
    4   green bell peppers, seeded, deveined, coarsely chopped
    1   (10-oz.) can tomatillos
    2   cups canned chopped roasted green chiles
    2   teaspoons ground coriander
    1   egg
        Salt and freshly ground black pepper, to taste
    3   tablespoons vegetable oil
  1/2   cup grated Parmesan cheese
   12   tortillas

1. Cook chicken in broth about 20 minutes. Shred meat and set aside, reserve broth.

2. In a large mixing bowl, beat cream cheese until smooth. Beat in 1/2 cup of cream, small amounts at a time. Stir in onions and chicken; mix well, and set aside.

3. Place bell peppers in blender or food processor. Add tomatillos, chopped green chiles, coriander and 1/4 cup reserved broth. Blend until smooth. Add remaining cream, egg, salt and pepper; blend 10 seconds.

4. Place mixture into a large bowl.

5. Preheat oven to 350F(175C).

Notes..
....
....
....

6. In a heavy 8- to 10-in. skillet, heat oil until very hot. Using tongs dip each tortilla in pepper mixture and carefully slide into the skillet. **Spattering will occur**. Fry for a minute or so on both sides until limp.

7. Transfer tortilla from skillet to a plate; place 1/4 cup chicken filling in the center. Fold one side of the tortilla over the filling and roll into a thick cylinder. Place seam side down in a 13 x 9-inch baking dish.

8. Pour remaining sauce over filled tortillas. Sprinkle with Parmesan cheese.

9. Bake in preheated oven about 20 minutes until cheese melts and enchiladas brown lightly on top. Serve at once.

Makes 6 servings.

Notes..
....
....
....

❧ CHICKEN FAJITAS ❧

---

  2 lbs. skinless, boned chicken breasts
  1 teaspoon peeled, grated fresh ginger
  2 garlic cloves, minced
  1 cup soy sauce
1/4 cup fresh orange juice
1/4 cup fresh lime juice
  2 tablespoons honey
  2 tablespoons olive oil or vegetable oil
  2 large white onions, sliced
1-1/2 green bell peppers, seeded, thinly sliced
1-1/2 red bell peppers, seeded, thinly sliced
    Salt, to taste
12 flour tortillas, warmed

SIDE DISHES
1/2 cup refried beans
  1 cup guacamole
  4 cups shredded lettuce
  1 cup grated Monterey Jack cheese
  1 cup dairy sour cream
    Salsa or chili sauce

1. Place a piece of waxed paper or plastic wrap on a cutting board. Place each chicken breast on top and cover with another piece of waxed paper or plastic wrap. With a mallet, flatten chicken breasts to 1/8-inch thick. Set aside.

2. In a large bowl, combine ginger, garlic, soy sauce, orange juice, lime juice and honey. Add chicken; refrigerate in marinade 3 to 6 hours.

3. About 10 minutes before cooking, drain chicken and pat dry. Grill or broil. Cook until no longer pink, but still moist, about 1-1/2 minutes per

Notes . . . .
. . . .
. . . .
. . . .

side. Remove from grill or broiler; slice cross grain into 1-1/4-inch strips; cover and set aside.

4. In a deep non-stick skillet, heat oil until very hot. Add onions and peppers; sauté. Add chicken strips and toss together. Season with salt to taste. Serve on a very hot plate, preferably a metal sizzle platter.

5. Serve with tortillas and side dishes.

Makes 6 servings.

> *Refried beans, guacamole, shredded lettuce, grated cheese, salsa or sauce should be prepared ahead of cooking chicken and be served as side dishes. Tortillas should be served hot in covered container.*
>
> *To assemble fajitas, place a portion of hot chicken mixture in center of the tortilla and top with the side dishes to taste. Fold tortilla, closing one end. Eat as hand food.*

Notes..
....
....
....

⋄{ CHICKEN RANCHERO }⋄

---

4 chicken breasts
3 large tomatoes, finely chopped
3 green chiles, roasted, peeled, seeded, finely chopped
1 onion, finely chopped
1 cup chicken broth
    Salt to taste
1 jalapeño, seeded, finely chopped
2 tablespoons all-purpose flour
3 tablespoons chili powder
3 tablespoons vegetable oil
2-1/2 cups water
1/2 teaspoon salt
2/3 cup grated Monterey Jack cheese

1. Poach chicken breasts in boiling, salted water 10 minutes.

2. Preheat oven to 450F(225C).

3. In saucepan, mix together tomatoes, green chiles, onion and chicken broth. Bring to a boil.

4. Cover and simmer 1/2 hour or until vegetables are soft.

5. Add salt, to taste, and jalapeño pepper.

6. In another pan, blend flour, chili powder and oil. Add water and salt, and bring to a boil. Simmer gently 5 minutes, stirring occasionally.

7. Pour sauce into a 9-inch-square baking dish and place chicken breasts on top of sauce.

8. Pour green chile and tomato sauce over the chicken breasts and sprinkle generously with grated cheese.

9. Bake uncovered 15-20 minutes, until chicken is tender and cheese is melted.

Makes 4 servings.

Notes..
....
....
....

❧ CHILE RELLENOS ❧

---

8   green chiles, roasted, peeled
1/2 lb. Longhorn, Cheddar or Monterey Jack cheese
3   cups oil for frying
1   cup all-purpose flour
1/2 teaspoon salt
1/2 teaspoon sugar
1   pinch of baking soda
1   egg
1/2 teaspoon oil
1   cup ice water
    Basic Red Sauce, page 129, or salsa

1. Make a small slit on the side of each chile pepper to remove the seeds and veins. Leave stem on chile. Cut cheese into 1-inch wide strips, the length of each chile, and 1/4 inch thick. Carefully insert a piece of cheese into each chile pepper. Pat dry and refrigerate for at least 30 minutes.

2. Heat 3 cups oil in deep skillet or deep-fryer to 375F(190C).

3. In a medium bowl, combine flour, salt, sugar, and baking soda. In a cup, beat egg, oil and cold water together with fork. Combine with flour mixture. Do not over mix. Use at once.

4. Dip chiles one at a time into batter. Allow excess batter to drip off. Slide coated chile gently into hot oil. Fry until golden brown on both sides. Drain on paper towels.

5. Serve immediately with red or green sauce or salsa on top.

Makes 4 servings.

✛ **VARIATION.** Substitute Picadillo, page 75, for cheese filling or combine the two for variety.

Notes..
....
....
....

❧ CHICKEN-FRIED STEAK ❧ WITH CREAM GRAVY

---

4 cups buttermilk
6 (7-oz.) round steaks
Salt and pepper, to taste
5 eggs
1 (12-oz.) can evaporated milk
1/2 cup vegetable oil
All-purpose flour
3 tablespoons all-purpose flour
2 cups water

1. Pound round steaks with a meat tenderizing mallet (or for best results, have your butcher run them through his tenderizing machine). Pour buttermilk into a shallow dish; add steaks and marinate at least 2 hours. Remove to a plate and discard buttermilk.

2. Sprinkle steak with salt and pepper; set aside. Beat eggs and 1/2 cup evaporated milk together in a bowl. Heat oil in a deep-sided skillet to 350F(175C).

3. Dredge steaks with flour; dip in the egg batter. Flour again lightly; shake off excess flour.

4. Add steaks to skillet one at a time; do not allow the temperature to drop. Fry 4 minutes, or until golden brown; turn to fry other side until golden brown. Remove from skillet; drain on paper towels. Keep warm in oven at 150F(65C).

5. Prepare gravy by pouring all but 4 teaspoons oil from skillet and reduce heat to low. Add 3 tablespoons flour to skillet; stirring constantly, cook until flour is brown.

6. Add remaining evaporated milk, whisking until smooth, scraping the bottom of the skillet to pick up all remaining material.

7. Add water gradually, stirring constantly, until gravy is smooth and thickened. Add salt and pepper to taste. Serve separately.

Makes 6 servings.

Notes ....
....
....

❧{ CHILE RELLENOS }❧ SAUSAGE CASSEROLE

　3　eggs
　1　cup evaporated milk
　1　tablespoon all-purpose flour
1/2　lb. pork sausage
　1　(4-oz.) can whole green New Mexican chiles
　1　cup grated Longhorn cheese
1/4　teaspoon paprika

1. Preheat oven to 350F(175C). Generously grease an 8-inch casserole.

2. In a bowl, beat eggs, milk and flour.

3. In skillet, brown sausage and pour off grease.

4. Drain chiles, split and layer in bottom of prepared casserole.

5. Top with sausage and cheese. Pour egg mixture over top. Sprinkle with paprika.

6. Bake in preheated oven, about 30 minutes, until top is firm and brown.

Makes 4 to 6 servings.

Notes..
....
....

❦ BEAN CHIMICHANGA ❧

6	large flour tortillas
12	tablespoons refried beans
6	tablespoons chopped, roasted, peeled, seeded, green chiles
12	tablespoons grated Longhorn cheese
1	cup dairy sour cream
12	tablespoons guacamole
	Salsa
1	cup shredded lettuce
1	cup peeled chopped tomatoes

1. Warm tortillas in a steamer or microwave.

2. In a small saucepan, heat beans and chiles.

3. In center of warm tortilla, spread refried beans and chile; sprinkle with cheese.

4. Fold edges of tortilla to center overlapping.

5. Place seam side down on a warmed serving plate; top with dairy sour cream.

6. Spoon guacamole on top of dairy sour cream.

7. Spoon salsa over ends.

8. Garnish with lettuce and tomatoes.

Makes 6 servings.

Arizonans call this a burro. *A* chimichanga *in Arizona would be deep-fried.*

Notes . . . .
. . . .
. . . .
. . . .

❧ GRILLED LAMB PATTIES ❧

---

    1   lb. ground lamb
    1   tablespoon vegetable oil
    6   tablespoons piñon nuts
  1/4   teaspoon ground coriander
  1/8   teaspoon ground cumin
    1   teaspoon chili powder
        Salt, to taste
  1/3   cup ice water

1. Place meat in a medium-size bowl.

2. In a small skillet, heat oil; sauté nuts in oil until they are lightly golden. Drain on paper towels.

3. Mix nuts, coriander, cumin and chili powder with meat. Add salt to taste.

4. Add ice water, a little at a time. Mix until all is incorporated.

5. Shape into 4 patties; refrigerate 2 hours before grilling.

6. Grill patties 5 minutes per side.

Makes 4 servings.

Notes..
....
....
....

❧ MEATBALLS ❧
IN CHILE SAUCE

---

  3 (6-inch) corn tortillas, cut in pieces
1/2 cup milk
1/2 lb. ground beef
1/2 lb. ground pork
1/2 lb. ground smoked ham
1/4 cup chopped onion
  1 garlic clove, finely chopped
  1 teaspoon ground cumin
  1 teaspoon dried-leaf oregano
     Salt and black pepper, to taste
  1 cup Basic Red Sauce, see page 129
  1 cup beef broth

1. Place tortilla pieces and milk in large bowl; let stand 15 minutes.

2. Mix in remaining ingredients, except for Basic Red Sauce and broth.

3. Shape meat mixture into 1-inch balls. In a skillet, brown meatballs on all sides. Remove and set aside.

4. Heat Basic Red Sauce and broth to boiling in 10-inch skillet; reduce heat. Add meatballs.

5. Cover, and simmer until done, 15 to 20 minutes.

Makes 6 servings.

Notes..
....
....
....

⊰{ MEXICAN CASSEROLE }⊱

1   lb. ground beef
1/2   chopped onion
    Salt and black pepper, to taste
1   (8-oz.) can kernel corn, drained
1   (4-oz.) can diced green chiles
1   (10-1/2-oz.) can cream of mushroom soup
8   corn tortillas
8   oz. shredded Cheddar cheese

1. Preheat oven to 350F(175C). Lightly grease a 2-quart casserole.

2. In a 10-inch skillet, brown meat and onion. Add salt and pepper to taste.

3. Add corn, green chiles and mushroom soup; mix well.

4. In prepared casserole, alternate layers of tortillas, meat mixture and cheese, ending with cheese on top.

5. Bake in preheated oven about 20 minutes, until brown and bubbly.

Makes 8 servings.

To reheat and soften tortillas, place on an ungreased surface and rub each lightly with a damp hand before heating a few seconds. Wrapping in a damp towel and heating in a microwave 20 seconds will also soften the tortilla.

Notes..
....
....
....

❧ PORK FAJITAS ❧

---

     2   lbs. pork tenderloin
   1/4   cup Ancho Mole Sauce, page 127
   1/2   cup freshly squeezed lemon juice
     4   garlic cloves, crushed
   1/4   teaspoon black peppercorns
     1   tablespoon water
 1-1/2   teaspoons salt, or to taste
    16   corn tortillas
     1   lemon, cut into wedges
     1   cup iceberg lettuce, shredded
     1   tomato, seeded, diced
   1/2   cup chopped onion
         Guacamole
         Dairy sour cream

1. Trim tenderloin of excess fat and all silver skin. In a deep bowl, mix mole sauce, lemon juice, garlic, peppercorns, and water. Place tenderloin in mixture to marinate. Cover with plastic and refrigerate overnight.

2. The following day, grill tenderloin until done, about 15 minutes, turning once or twice during grilling. For a special flavor, use mesquite wood chips in the fire. For best results, allow meat to rest 10 minutes before slicing. Or, bake tenderloin uncovered in oven at 450F(230C), 20 to 25 minutes.

3. Before serving, wrap tortillas in foil and heat in 275F(135C) oven. To serve, place strips of the tenderloin down the center of warmed tortillas and top with remaining garnishes, to taste.

Makes 8 servings.

Notes...
....
....
....

❧ PICADILLO OVER RICE ❧

1/2   lb. ground beef
1/2   lb. ground pork
  1   cup chopped onion
  2   garlic cloves, minced
  1   (16-oz.) can tomatoes, chopped
  1   tablespoon vinegar
  1   pinch of salt
1/2   teaspoon ground cinnamon
  1   pinch ground cloves
1/4   teaspoon ground cumin
  1   teaspoon salt
  1   bay leaf
1/8   teaspoon Tabasco® sauce
1/2   cup seedless raisins
1/2   cup green olives, chopped
1/2   cup blanched slivered almonds
      Cooked rice

1. In a 10-inch skillet, stir meats over high heat. When meats begin to cook, add onion and garlic.

2. When meat browns, pour off excess fat; add remaining ingredients except raisins, olives and almonds.

3. Reduce heat to simmer; cover and cook 30 minutes.

4. Add water if necessary. Picadillo should be moist, but not soupy.

5. Add raisins, olives and almonds; continue cooking 10 minutes.

6. Serve over cooked rice.

Makes 4 servings.

Special Note: Picadillo is an excellent filling for tacos, tamales, and green or red chile rellenos. If used for filling, meat should be shredded after cooking.

Notes...
....
....
....

⌊ ROUND STEAK ROLLS ⌋

1-1/2 lbs. round steak, cut 1/4-inch thick
Salt and black pepper, to taste
3 green chiles, roasted, peeled, seeded, cut into halves
1/4 cup butter or oil
1 garlic clove, minced
2 cups fresh bread crumbs
3 tablespoons chopped parsley
2 hard-cooked eggs, chopped
1/4 cup Parmesan cheese
1/4 cup butter or oil
1 (10-1/2-oz.) can condensed onion soup
1/2 cup chopped fresh mushrooms
1 cup dry red wine
Cooked noodles

1. Pound steak until very thin; cut into six long pieces and sprinkle with salt and pepper.

2. Place halved chiles over strips of meat.

3. In a small skillet, heat 1/4 cup butter, sauté garlic until golden brown. Add crumbs and sauté until golden. Stir in parsley, hard-cooked eggs and Parmesan cheese.

4. Spoon mixture onto each piece of meat. Roll up and fasten with toothpicks.

5. In a large skillet, heat remaining 1/4 cup butter, brown meat on all sides.

6. Add onion soup, mushrooms and wine. Cover and simmer 1 hour, or until meat is tender.

7. Serve with noodles.

Makes 6 servings.

Notes..
....
....
....

❧{ SOUTHWEST RIBLETS }❧

1/2 cup chopped onion
  2 tablespoons vegetable oil
  1 tablespoon ground red chiles
  6 dried juniper berries, crushed
  3 garlic cloves, finely chopped
1/2 teaspoon salt
1/2 oz. bitter-baking chocolate, grated
  1 cup water
  2 tablespoons cider vinegar
  1 (6-oz.) can tomato paste
  2 cups sugar
  3 lbs. pork back ribs, cut lengthwise across bones

1. In a 2-quart saucepan, cook and stir onion in oil 2 minutes. Stir in ground red chiles, juniper berries, garlic and salt. Cover and cook 5 minutes, stirring occasionally.

2. Stir in chocolate until melted.

3. Pour water, vinegar and tomato paste into food processor; blend until smooth.

4. Add onion mixture and sugar; cover and process until well blended.

5. Heat oven to 375F(190C).

6. Cut between ribs to separate. Place in a single layer in roasting pan; pour sauce evenly over pork.

7. Bake uncovered 30 minutes; turn ribs and bake until done, about 30 minutes longer.

Makes 6 servings.

Notes..
....
....
....

❧ STUFFED MEXICAN ❧ CABBAGE

---

      1   medium head cabbage
    1/2   lb. pork sausage
      1   lb. ground beef
      1   onion, grated
  1-1/2   cups chopped, roasted, peeled, seeded green chile peppers
    1/2   teaspoon garlic salt
  1-1/2   cups thinly sliced, peeled, apples
      1   onion, chopped
      1   (16-oz.) can sauerkraut, rinsed, drained
      1   cup chicken broth
      1   cup tomato juice

1. Core cabbage. Place in a large pot and cover with boiling water; simmer 5 minutes. Remove cabbage from water and cool. Pull leaves off one at a time; you should have about 10 large leaves. Trim away vein end of leaves.

2. In a skillet, combine sausage and ground beef and cook 15 to 20 minutes. Add grated onion and cook until onion is clear. Drain off excess fat. Add green chiles and garlic salt; mix well. Cool.

3. Place 1/3 cup of meat and chile mixture near the vein end of leaf. Fold the end over the stuffing; fold over the sides, envelope-fashion, and roll as tightly as possible.

4. Preheat oven to 350F(175C). In a bowl, mix apples, chopped onion and sauerkraut. Spread half of this mixture on bottom of deep baking dish or casserole. Place cabbage rolls on sauerkraut. Spread remaining mixture on top.

5. Mix broth and tomato juice, pour over rolls. Cover and bake in preheated oven 1 hour.

Makes 4 to 5 servings.

Notes..
....
....
....

VEGETABLES & SIDE DISHES

New Mexico's vast irrigated farms grow a large variety of vegetables. The chile pepper reigns supreme here and is considered a vegetable, not just a spice. An impressive number of dishes contain chile peppers used in every possible way. I've been known to send packages of fresh chile peppers to people who had once lived here and are now deprived of this basic ingredient. I encourage you to use fresh chile peppers whenever possible.

I hope you'll try both of my squash recipes, because each offers new combinations that I think you will find exciting to taste. Peanut-Stuffed Acorn Squash makes a delightful brunch entrée or the perfect side dish for succulent roast pork or ham.

Of course, I am including a recipe for Pinto Beans that gives you choices of cooking methods. To guarantee having tender beans, remember to add salt to beans after they have cooked. You can use this versatile ingredient as the basis for numerous dishes, for soups, salads, or main dishes. What a delicious, healthful extender.

❧ FRIED TOMATILLOS ❧

2-1/4 lbs. fresh tomatillos
1/4 cup olive oil or peanut oil
2 onions, quartered, thinly sliced
1 teaspoon salt
2/3 cup whipping cream
12 corn or flour tortillas, warmed
Salsa
1 cup shredded Longhorn cheese

1. Remove outer husks from tomatillos. Rinse and cut in half. Cut into thin slices.

2. Heat oil in large skillet until very hot. Add onions and stir to coat well. Add tomatillos and salt; cook until tomatillos are soft.

3. Add cream and bring to a boil. Immediately remove from heat.

4. To serve, spoon about 1/2 cup tomatillo mixture on each tortilla. Top with salsa and shredded cheese.

Makes 4 servings.

Notes..
....
....
....

ᐧᢶ{ CAULIFLOWER & PECANS }ᢶᐧ

1 1/2　cups cauliflowerets
　3/4　cup mayonnaise
　1/2　cup dairy sour cream
　　4　tablespoons drained horseradish
　1/2　teaspoon prepared mustard
　3/4　cup sliced green bell pepper
　　1　cup chopped celery
　　1　cup coarsely grated carrots
　　1　cup toasted whole pecans
　　　　Salt and black pepper, to taste
　　　　Lettuce leaves

1. Blanch cauliflowerets in hot salted water 2 minutes; drain and remove to a bowl. Cover and chill.

2. In a small bowl, combine mayonnaise, sour cream, horseradish and mustard.

3. In a salad bowl, combine chilled cauliflowerets with bell pepper, celery, carrots, and pecans.

4. Pour dressing over all, toss together to coat. Season with salt and black pepper, to taste.

5. Line salad plates with lettuce; serve salad on lettuce.

Makes 4 servings.

Notes..
....
....
....

❧{ BLACK BEANS WITH }❧ CHILES & TOMATOES

2	cups cooked black beans
2	tablespoons vegetable oil
1/2	onion, chopped
1	garlic clove
1	fresh tomato, peeled, seeded, chopped
1/4	cup chopped, roasted, peeled, seeded, green chiles
1/4	teaspoon ground cumin
	Salt and black pepper, to taste

1. In a saucepan, heat beans and 1/2 cup of their liquid to a simmer.

2. In a small skillet, heat oil. Add onion and garlic; cook over low heat until onion is soft.

3. Add remaining ingredients, except beans, and increase heat. Simmer over medium heat 2 minutes, stirring as needed.

4. Place 1/2 cup in a food processor or blender and purée.

5. Pour puréed mixture into saucepan with beans. Simmer slowly about 5 minutes. Serve at once.

Makes 4 servings.

Notes..
....
....
....

❧ PEANUT-STUFFED ❧ ACORN SQUASH

2   acorn squash
2   tablespoons butter
2   cups minced baked ham
2   tablespoons minced onion
1   tablespoon packed brown sugar
1   tablespoon grated orange peel
1/4 cup orange juice
1   teaspoon salt
1   cup chopped unsalted peanuts
1/2 cup melted butter
1/2 cup packed brown sugar
1/2 cup unsalted peanuts

1. Preheat oven to 350F(175C). Lightly grease a shallow baking pan.

2. Cut squash in half and remove seeds.

3. Place cut side down on prepared pan. Bake 45 minutes, or until tender.

4. Remove from oven and scoop pulp into a bowl, leaving a thin shell intact.

5. In a large skillet, heat 2 tablespoons butter, sauté ham and onion. Stir in squash pulp, 1 tablespoon brown sugar, orange peel, orange juice and salt. Stir in 1 cup peanuts.

6. Fill squash shells with ham and squash mixture. Drizzle tops with melted butter; sprinkle with brown sugar and peanuts.

7. Place filled shells on a baking pan and return to oven. Bake 20 to 30 minutes until thoroughly heated.

Makes 4 servings.

Valencia peanuts from Portales, New Mexico have become a major crop. We are finding a great number of recipes that use peanuts.

Notes..
....
....
....

❧ INDIAN SQUASH ❧

2   tablespoons butter
1   small onion, chopped
2   garlic cloves, minced
2   or 3 yellow crookneck squash, 1/4-inch-thick slices
2   fresh tomatoes, peeled, chopped
1   (16-oz.) can kernel corn, drained
1/2 teaspoon salt
3   tablespoons chopped, roasted, peeled, seeded green chiles
1/4 teaspoon dried-leaf oregano
1/2 teaspoon black pepper
1   cup light cream
1/4 teaspoon Tabasco sauce
1   (3-oz.) pkg. cream cheese, cut in cubes

1. In a heavy skillet, melt butter; add onion and garlic, sauté about 5 minutes.

2. Add squash to skillet, continue cooking another 5 minutes, stirring occasionally. Add tomatoes, corn, salt, chile peppers, oregano and black pepper. Reduce heat to low, cook about 20 minutes, until squash is tender. Stir as needed.

3. Stir in light cream, Tabasco sauce and cream cheese. Cook until cream cheese is melted and sauce is heated through. Serve at once.

Makes 4 servings.

Notes..
....
....
....

❧ TRIPLE CORN CASSEROLE ❧

2 cups shredded Colby cheese
2 eggs, beaten
1 (16-oz.) can cream-style corn
1/2 cup chopped, roasted, peeled, seeded, fresh green chiles or canned
1 (16-oz.) can kernel corn, drained, or fresh or frozen corn
1 cup cornmeal
1/2 teaspoon baking powder
1/2 teaspoon salt

1. Preheat oven to 350F(175C). Grease a 2-quart casserole dish.

2. Divide cheese in half and set aside. In a bowl, mix eggs, cream-style corn, green chile peppers, kernel corn and 1 cup cheese together.

3. In a separate bowl, stir together cornmeal, baking powder and salt.

4. Mix cornmeal mixture into egg mixture. Spoon into prepared dish and top with remaining cheese.

5. Bake, covered, in preheated oven 30 minutes or until firm and lightly browned.

Makes 4 servings.

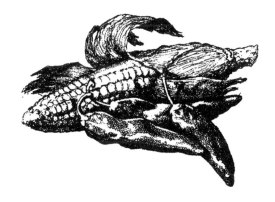

Notes..
....
....
....

❧ FRESH-CORN SAUTÉ ❧

- 2 tablespoons olive oil
- 3 cups fresh corn kernels
- 1 New Mexican green chile, roasted, peeled, seeded
- 1 red bell pepper
- 3 green onions with tops, thinly sliced
- 1/3 cup skim milk
- 1/4 cup fresh minced cilantro
- 1/2 teaspoon freshly ground black pepper
- Cilantro

1. Heat olive oil in a large non-stick skillet, sauté corn 1 minute. Stir in chile pepper, bell pepper; add green onions, including tops, and sauté about 1 minute.

2. Add milk, cover and simmer about 2 minutes. Uncover and cook, stirring constantly, over high heat until liquid evaporates.

3. Stir in minced fresh cilantro and black pepper.

4. Garnish with additional fresh cilantro. Serve immediately.

Makes 6 servings.

Each year in Albuquerque, the National Fiery Foods Show is held in mid-February. Buyers, manufacturers, and assorted fiery-food fans meet to do business and have a hot time. More than 6,000 people taste and buy a wide variety of hot and spicy foods each year.

Notes...
....
....
....

⊰ CHILE EGGPLANT ⊱

Oil for frying
2　eggs, beaten
1/4　cup milk
1　large eggplant, peeled and sliced crosswise into 1/4-inch-pieces
1　cup toasted bread crumbs
2　cups canned stewed tomatoes
2　cups roasted, peeled, diced green chiles
1　large white onion, diced
1　lb. Longhorn cheese, grated

1. Preheat oven to 350F(175C). Heat oil in a large skillet.

2. Combine beaten eggs with milk.

3. Dip eggplant slices into egg-milk mixture, then into bread crumbs. Fry in hot oil until golden brown on both sides.

4. Place 1/2 eggplant slices in bottom of ungreased 13 x 9-inch casserole.

5. Spread half of stewed tomatoes over eggplant, then 1/2 each of chiles, diced onion and grated cheese.

6. Repeat with a second layer.

7. Cover and bake in preheated oven 1 hour. Uncover and bake an additional 1/2 hour.

Makes 6 servings.

> *For variety, use other cheeses. Blend Monterey Jack, Longhorn, Mozzarella or Cheddar in various combinations to suit your taste.*

Notes..
....
....
....

❧ POTATO QUICHE ❧

---

1   (32-oz.) pkg. frozen "Southern-style" hash-brown
      potatoes, thawed
1   cup salsa
1/4   cup ranch dressing
4   eggs, lightly beaten
1   cup milk
2   (4-oz.) cans diced green chile peppers
1   cup shredded Monterey Jack cheese
1   cup shredded Cheddar cheese
    Sour Cream
    Salsa
    Fresh cilantro

1. Preheat oven to 450F(230C). Spray a 13 x 9-inch baking dish with a vegetable cooking spray. Set aside.

2. Line a large bowl with several layers of paper towels. Place potatoes in bowl, cover with 2 layers of paper towels and press to remove excess moisture.

3. Spread potatoes evenly in bottom of prepared baking dish; bake in preheated oven 45 minutes or until golden brown.

4. In a small bowl, blend salsa with ranch dressing. In another bowl, mix eggs and milk.

5. When potatoes are cooked, remove from oven. Reduce heat to

Notes..
....
....
....

350F(175C). Spread salsa mixture over potatoes. Pour egg mixture over salsa.

6. Sprinkle chile peppers over eggs; top with a layer of Monterey Jack cheese and then Cheddar cheese.

7. Return to oven and bake 45 minutes, or until cheese bubbles and is browned. Let stand 5 minutes before serving.

8. Top each serving with sour cream, salsa and cilantro.

Makes 8 servings.

Notes..
....
....
....

❧ MARINATED ONIONS ❧

3 large red onions, sliced
1/2 cup vegetable oil
2 tablespoons lemon juice
2 tablespoons chopped, roasted, peeled, green chiles
1/2 teaspoon garlic salt
1/2 teaspoon salt
1/2 teaspoon paprika
1/2 teaspoon sugar
1/4 cup crumbled blue cheese

1. Place red onions in a large bowl.

2. In a cup, combine remaining ingredients, except cheese. Stir well and pour over onions. Toss to coat.

3. Sprinkle cheese over onions; mix together. Cover and refrigerate 24 to 36 hours.

Makes 4 to 6 servings.

Notes...
....
....
....

⊰{ SWEET POTATOES }⊱ & CHILES

1/2 cup vegetable oil
2 lbs. sweet potatoes, peeled, diced
2 New Mexican chile peppers, peeled, seeded, deveined, chopped
1 (8-oz.) pkg. cream cheese, softened
12 corn or flour tortillas, crisped or warmed
Salsa
Fresh cilantro, chopped

1. Divide oil between 2 large skillets and heat until very hot.

2. Divide sweet potatoes evenly between skillets; stir to coat. Spread into even layers and cook about 10 minutes.

3. Turn potatoes over; add chiles in an even layer over potatoes. Continue cooking, about 20 minutes, stirring occasionally. Potatoes should be browned on all sides.

4. Distribute cream cheese over potatoes. Cover and cook 2 to 3 minutes, until cheese melts.

5. Spoon about 1/3 cup potatoes into center of each tortilla. Top with salsa and cilantro. Fold and serve.

Makes 4 to 6 servings.

Notes...
....
....
....

⊰ PINTO BEANS ⊱

2-1/2 cups dried pinto beans
   1 garlic clove, crushed
     Water
     Salt and black pepper, to taste
     Chili sauce
     Grated cheese

1. Rinse beans and remove any dirt, debris, or broken beans.

2. Place rinsed, sorted beans in a large pot. Cover with water and bring to a boil. Boil 2 minutes; remove from heat and let stand 1 hour. Drain water, refill pan with fresh water.

> **Stove-top method**: To soaked beans add garlic. Simmer, covered, over low heat, about 2 hours, or until tender.

> **Crock-pot method**: Place rinsed, sorted beans and water 4 times the amount of beans into pot. Cook on high 8 to 10 hours. Beans will have absorbed water and expanded. The water level should barely cover the beans. If water is needed, add only hot or boiling water in small amounts. The beans are done when they are soft with most retaining their shape. At this point, you can add salt to taste.

> **Pressure-cooker method**, see page 12.

3. Serve plain or topped with chili sauce, and sprinkle with grated cheese.

Makes 6 servings.

For added flavor, we always add a couple of table-spoons of sugar to cooked beans. To thicken the juice, mash some beans and stir into the pot.

Notes ....
....
....
....

SANTA FE CINNAMON RICE

---

4   tablespoons unsalted butter
1/2   cup diced carrots
1/2   cup diced celery
1/2   cup diced onion
2   cups converted long-grain rice
    Salt, to taste
4   cinnamon sticks or 1 teaspoon ground cinnamon
1/2   cup currants
6   cups water

1. Over medium heat, melt 2 tablespoons of butter in a deep saucepan.

2. Add carrots, celery and onion. Cover, and cook over low heat, stirring occasionally, 10 minutes.

3. Stir in rice, salt, cinnamon, currants and water. Bring mixture to boil over high heat.

4. When water has reduced down to the level of the rice, turn heat to low; cover, and continue to cook 15 to 20 minutes, stirring occasionally.

5. Remove cinnamon sticks; add remaining butter, and season with salt, to taste.

Makes 6 servings.

This recipe was a prize winner in a national contest that required rice to be the main ingredient.

Notes..
....
....
....

❖ CALABACITAS ❖

---

3   tablespoons butter
3   medium zucchini, cubed
1/2 cup chopped onion
1/2 cup sliced, roasted, peeled, green chiles
2   cups kernel corn
1   cup milk
1/2 cup grated Monterey or Jack cheese

1. In a large skillet, heat butter; sauté zucchini and onion until tender.

2. Add chiles, corn and milk. Simmer mixture 15 to 20 minutes to blend flavors. Add cheese and heat until melted.

Makes 4 servings.

For information about the International Connoisseurs of Green and Red Chili, write to the World Headquarters, Box 3467, Las Cruces, NM 88003.

Notes...
....
....
....

CHILI

There is no question that one of New Mexico's major contributions to American cuisine is chili. No one knows for sure who first combined meat and peppers, the main ingredients of chili. Some New Mexicans claim it was a chuckwagon cook who ran out of black pepper. Looking for a substitute, he tried the little red peppers commonly used by local Indians and Mexicans. Thus, chili was born.

When I visit chili cookoffs in the Southwest, I find a warm group of people, cutting across all ethnic and economic lines. They graciously share their love of chili with anyone willing to stop and sample their culinary efforts. They believe, as I do, that the best chili is the finest example of the melding of flavor and heat. In the following recipes I have included some that are simple and easy, as well as some that could be entered in a chili contest. Remember—*chile* spelled with an "*e*" is a variety of pepper; *chili* spelled with an "*i*" is a mixture of meats, spices and chiles.

❧ ALBUQUERQUE ❧ OKTOBERFEST CHILI

1/3 cup olive or vegetable oil
3 lbs. lean beef, cut into 1-inch cubes
2 onions, finely chopped
3 garlic cloves, finely chopped
 Salt, to taste
4 cups boiling water
1 teaspoon caraway seeds
2 teaspoons sesame seeds
1/2 teaspoon ground oregano
1 tablespoon ground hot red chile pepper
2 tablespoons ground mild chile peppers
1 cup pitted green olives
2 (16-oz.) cans kidney beans, drained
 Salt and pepper, to taste

1. Heat olive oil in a 6-quart Dutch oven or heavy pot over medium heat. Add beef cubes a few at a time, stirring to brown evenly. As beef browns, remove from pan and set aside.

2. After beef is browned, add onions and garlic to pan and cook until soft.

3. Return beef cubes to the pan and season with salt. Add boiling water, caraway seeds, sesame seeds and oregano. Bring to a boil, reduce heat and simmer uncovered 1 hour.

4. Slowly add ground chile, tasting until you get the degree of hotness and flavor you prefer.

5. Add olives and simmer covered an additional 45 minutes to 1 hour.

6. Taste and adjust seasonings to taste. Add kidney beans and heat thoroughly.

Makes 6 servings.

Notes..
....
....
....

❧ CHICKEN & WHITE ❧ BEAN CHILI

1/4   cup butter
1   large white onion, chopped
1   garlic clove, finely chopped
4   cups cooked chicken, cut into 1-inch cubes
3   cups chicken broth
2   tablespoons chopped fresh cilantro
1   tablespoon dried-leaf basil
2   teaspoons dried red chile, ground
1/4   teaspoon ground cloves
2   cups cooked Great Northern beans, or 2 (16-oz.) cans, drained
3/4   cup chopped tomato
      Tortilla chips

1. In a 4-quart Dutch oven or heavy pot, heat butter; add onion and garlic; cook until soft.

2. Add remaining ingredients, except for tomato and tortilla chips.

3. Bring to a boil and reduce heat. Cover and simmer 1 hour, stirring occasionally.

4. Serve with tomatoes over top, and tortilla chips.

Makes 6 servings.

Notes...
....
....
....

❧ CHAMPIONSHIP CHILI ❧

3/4   cup all-purpose flour
1   tablespoon salt
1/2   teaspoon black pepper
1   lb. lean pork shoulder, cut into 1/2-inch cubes
2   lbs. lean beef shoulder, cut into 1/2-inch cubes
3   tablespoons vegetable oil
3   onions, chopped
6   garlic cloves, minced
6   cups beef broth
4   dried ancho peppers
1   mild, fresh green chile pepper, roasted, seeded
1   cascabel pepper, roasted, seeded
   Ground cumin and salt, to taste
1/4   cup water

1. Combine flour, salt and pepper in a paper bag.

2. Add meat to bag and shake to coat. Save remaining flour.

3. Place oil in a Dutch oven or heavy pot. Heat at high temperature until oil smokes. Add meat; stir constantly to prevent sticking.

4. Add onions and garlic. Cook and stir until soft.

5. Add beef broth and bring to a boil. Reduce heat and simmer.

6. Wash peppers under cold, running water; remove stems, seeds and devein. Place in saucepan and cover with water. Boil 5 minutes, then steep 10 to 15 minutes.

Notes..
....
....
....

7. Remove peppers with slotted spoon; purée in food processor with 1-1/2 cups chile cooking water.

8. Add purée to meat. Cover and simmer 2 to 3 hours, or until meat is tender. Add cumin and salt to taste.

9. Mix reserved flour from bag and 1/4 cup of cold water. Stir into chili and cook 3 to 5 minutes to thicken chili.

Makes 8 servings.

For information about the International Chili Society, write to: International Chili Society, P.O. Box 2966, Newport Beach, CA 92663

Notes..
....
....
....

❧ CHILI COLORADO ❧

---

     4   oz. dried New Mexico chiles
     3   cups water
   1/2   cup olive or vegetable oil
     2   large onions, chopped
     3   garlic cloves, minced
     5   lbs. boneless chuck, cut into 1-inch cubes
   1/2   cup all-purpose flour
     1   (14-1/2-oz.) can beef broth
   1/4   cup fresh cilantro, chopped
     2   teaspoons each of ground cumin, ground cloves,
            dried-leaf oregano, tarragon and rosemary
     2   (28-oz.) cans tomatoes

1. Rinse chiles; discard stems and seeds. Break chiles into pieces. Combine chile pieces and water in a 2-1/2-quart saucepan. Bring to a boil over high heat; reduce heat, cover and simmer, until chiles are soft, about 30 minutes.

2. In a blender or food processor, purée chiles with their liquid. Rub purée through a fine strainer and discard residue.

3. Heat oil in a 6- to 8-quart Dutch oven or heavy pot over medium heat. Add onions and garlic; cook, stirring often, until onions are soft. Sprinkle meat with flour. Add meat and chile purée to pan and cook, stirring, 5 minutes.

4. Add broth, cilantro, cumin, cloves, oregano, tarragon, rosemary, and tomatoes with their liquid. Reduce heat and simmer, uncovered, stirring often, until meat is very tender, 3 to 4 hours.

Makes 10 servings.

Notes..
....
....
....

⊰{ COWPOKE CHILI }⊱

---

   1 lb. slab bacon
   2 lbs. dry pinto or navy beans
   1 large onion, sliced
   4 garlic cloves, sliced
  12 cups water
   1 (16-oz.) can tomatoes
   2 ancho peppers, roasted, peeled, seeded, deveined
   2 serrano peppers, roasted, peeled, seeded deveined, or
 1/2 tablespoon chili powder
2-1/2 teaspoons salt
   1 teaspoon coriander seeds, crushed
  12 canned serrano peppers

1. Remove rind from the bacon. Cut rind into 1/2-inch squares. Cut bacon into small pieces and set aside.

2. Put rind, beans, onions and garlic into a kettle. Add water and bring to boil. Lower heat, cover and cook beans gently about 1-1/2 hours.

3. Uncover and cook 15 minutes.

4. In a separate pan, fry reserved diced bacon until slightly crisp. Add tomatoes and remaining ingredients to bacon. Cook over medium heat about 10 minutes. Skim off fat.

5. Add bacon and tomato mixture to the beans. Continue cooking over low heat about 1 hour, or until beans are tender.

Makes 6 servings.

Notes..
....
....
....

❦ FRUIT & NUT CHILI ❧

1-1/2 lbs. lean ground beef
   2 cups chopped onions
   3 garlic cloves, minced
   2 (16-oz.) cans tomatoes, cut up
   1 (15-oz.) can tomato sauce
   1 (14-1/2-oz.) can chicken broth
   3 bell peppers, chopped
   2 (4-oz.) cans diced green chiles
   2 cooking apples, peeled, cored, chopped
   3 tablespoons chili powder
   2 tablespoons unsweetened cocoa powder
   1 tablespoon curry powder
   1 teaspoon ground cinnamon
   1 (15-oz.) can red kidney beans, drained
 2/3 cup each slivered almonds, raisins, shredded cheddar
     cheese and yogurt or dairy sour cream

1. In a large Dutch oven or heavy pot, cook beef, onions and garlic until meat is brown. Drain off fat.

2. Stir in tomatoes with liquid, tomato sauce, chicken broth, bell peppers, green chile peppers, apples, chili powder, cocoa, curry and cinnamon. Bring to a boil and reduce heat. Cover and simmer 1 hour.

3. Add kidney beans and almonds. Heat through.

4. Serve topped with raisins, cheddar cheese, and yogurt or dairy sour cream.

Makes 8 servings.

Notes...
....
....
....

❈{ GRINGO CHILI }❈

2	teaspoons vegetable oil
1/2	medium onion, coarsely chopped
1	lb. lean beef, coarsely ground
1	tablespoon ground chile, mild
1	(4-oz.) can chopped green chiles
1/4	teaspoon dried-leaf oregano
3/4	teaspoon ground cumin
2	garlic cloves, finely chopped
2	(10-1/2-oz.) cans tomato soup
1	(10-1/2-oz.) can onion soup
1	(16-oz.) can pinto beans, drained

1. In a large Dutch oven or heavy pot, heat oil. Add onion and cook until soft.

2. Combine meat with ground chile, green chiles, oregano, cumin and garlic. Break up with fork and cook, stirring frequently until meat is brown.

3. Add tomato soup, onion soup, and pinto beans. Bring to a rolling boil; reduce heat and simmer, uncovered, until chili mixture thickens to desired consistency.

Makes 4 servings.

> *Christopher Columbus is credited with the "discovery" of chile peppers on his first voyage to the New World. His journal reported its use by the natives as a principal food. He introduced the chile to the Old World by taking seeds back to Europe.*

Notes...
....
....
....

⚜{ JOSE'S FAST CHILI }⚜

---

    3   tablespoons vegetable oil
    1   lb. ground beef
    1   large onion, finely chopped
2-1/2   cups cooked pinto beans
    1   (15-oz.) can tomato sauce
    1   teaspoon salt
    1   tablespoon all-purpose flour
2-1/2   tablespoons chili powder, recipe below
    3   tablespoons water

1. Heat oil in a large skillet, and cook meat until slightly brown.

2. Add onion, and cook until onion is soft.

3. Add beans, undrained, and tomato sauce. Cook over medium heat 15 minutes, stirring frequently.

4. In a separate bowl, combine salt, flour, chili powder and water.

5. Add mixture to meat and cover. Simmer 1 hour, stirring occasionally.

Makes 6 servings.

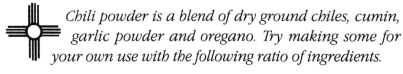 *Chili powder is a blend of dry ground chiles, cumin, garlic powder and oregano. Try making some for your own use with the following ratio of ingredients.*

CHILI POWDER
    7   tablespoons ground chile powder
    2   tablespoons garlic powder
1-1/2   tablespoons ground cumin
1-1/2   tablespoons ground oregano

Using various types of dried chili powder can give you unusual taste treats.

Notes..
....
....
....

⸙ MESILLA VALLEY CHILI ⸙

2   lbs. coarsely ground beef
4   tablespoons Mesilla Valley or other chili-powder mix
2   garlic cloves
4   tablespoons all-purpose flour
4   tablespoons vegetable oil
1   chopped onion
1   teaspoon salt
4   cups hot water

1. In a medium-size bowl, mix together meat, chili powder mix, garlic and flour.

2. In a large heavy skillet, heat oil over medium heat; add onion and sauté until tender.

3. Add meat to skillet and cook until meat is browned. Add salt.

4. Slowly add water and simmer 1 hour, or until tender.

Makes 4 servings.

Mesilla Valley produces chili mixes of all heats, to suit your taste; or you may substitute the chili-powder mix that is available.

Prices are available from: Mesilla Valley Seasons, 812 Solano Drive, Las Cruces, NM 88005

Mesilla is located 2 miles south of Las Cruces, NM, on a little piece of land that rises above the Rio Grande river. Settled in 1850, this farming community is in the heart of New Mexico's chile-growing activities. It is also the home of the famous La Posta restaurant and artists' shops.

Notes..
....
....
....

❧ NEW MEXICO ❧ GREEN CHILI

2 tablespoons vegetable oil
1/3 cup all-purpose flour
3 lbs. lean, boneless pork shoulder, cut into 1/2-inch cubes
3 onions, coarsely chopped
4 garlic cloves, chopped
2 (16-oz.) cans whole green chiles, drained, seeded, cut
   into 2-inch slices
2 (16-oz.) cans whole tomatoes
3 cups water
2 teaspoons salt
1/2 teaspoon dried-leaf oregano

1. Heat oil in a heavy skillet. Place flour in a small paper bag; add pork cubes and shake to coat with flour. Add pork to oil, a few cubes at a time, and brown evenly. Remove the browned pork and place in a 5-quart Dutch oven or heavy pot. Continue cooking a few at a time until all are browned.

2. Add onions and garlic to skillet, and cook until soft, stirring occasionally. Remove from heat and add to Dutch oven with browned pork.

3. Stir all remaining ingredients into pot with pork. Bring mixture to boil; reduce heat and cook uncovered, about 45 minutes. Taste and adjust seasonings; cook an additional 1/2 hour longer.

Makes 6 servings.

Notes..
....
....
....

❧ QUICK-&-EASY CHILI ❧ WITH BEANS

1/4 cup vegetable oil
3 lbs. lean, coarsely ground beef
2 small green peppers, chopped
2 medium onions, thinly sliced
2 garlic cloves, crushed
3 (16-oz.) cans whole tomatoes
3 tablespoons chili powder
2 teaspoons crushed cumin seeds
1/4 teaspoon Tabasco sauce
1 cup water
3 (15-oz.) cans pinto or kidney beans

1. Heat oil in a large Dutch oven or heavy pot. Cook beef, green peppers, onions and garlic in oil until beef is lightly browned.

2. Add all remaining ingredients, except beans. Cover and simmer 45 minutes.

3. Stir in the undrained beans. Cover and simmer 25 minutes.

Makes 4 servings.

There are more historic, prehistoric, human and scenic interests in New Mexico than any other similar area in the world, not excepting India, Europe or Asia.

Notes..
....
....
....

⊰{ RIO GRANDE RED }⊱

---

2   tablespoons vegetable oil
1   large onion, coarsely chopped
3   lbs. lean, coarsely ground beef
3   garlic cloves, finely chopped
4   tablespoons ground hot red chile peppers
4   tablespoons ground mild red chile peppers
2   teaspoons ground cumin
3   cups water
1-1/2 teaspoons salt

1. Heat oil in a large Dutch oven or large heavy pot over medium heat. Add onion and cook until soft.

2. Combine the meat with garlic, ground chile and cumin. Add meat and spice mixture to pot. Break up lumps with a fork; cook, stirring occasionally, until the meat is browned.

3. Stir in water and salt. Bring to a boil; reduce heat and simmer, uncovered, about 2-1/2 to 3 hours. Stir mixture occasionally; cook until meat is tender and flavors are well blended. Add more water if necessary.

Makes 6 servings.

HABANERO CHILE PEPPER
Sometimes called the Scot's Bonnet—*or the* Bahamian—*this chile is the world's hottest. It is the most sought-after of all chile peppers. Lovers of this hot variety claim its taste is unmistakable.*

Notes..
....
....
....

⊰{ SWEET CHILI }⊱

---

  1 lb. lean ground beef
  1 large white onion, minced
  1 (8-oz.) can tomato sauce
  1 cup refried beans, or 1 (16-oz.) can
  1 cup kidney beans, or 1 (16-oz.) can, drained
  1 cup water
1/4 cup finely chopped celery
1/4 green bell pepper, finely chopped
1/4 teaspoon hot red chili powder
     Salt and black pepper, to taste
  1 teaspoon paprika
1/8 teaspoon garlic salt
  2 teaspoons mild chili powder
1/4 teaspoon Worcestershire sauce
1/8 teaspoon prepared mustard
1/2 teaspoon brown sugar
1/2 teaspoon molasses

1. In a Dutch oven or heavy 6-quart pan, brown beef with onion and drain off fat.

2. Combine remaining ingredients and simmer at least 2 hours.

Makes 4 servings.

Notes..
....
....
....

⊰{ SIX-PEPPER CHILI }⊱

---

2   tablespoons vegetable oil

3   lbs. lean stew beef, cut in 1/2-inch cubes

1   lb. pork loin, cut in 1/2-inch cubes

3   large onions, finely chopped

1   tablespoon ground cumin

7   garlic cloves

1   tablespoon ground chile peppers

1   teaspoon Tabasco sauce

2   teaspoons salt

5   jalapeño peppers seeded, deveined

1   lb. fresh or canned tomatoes

7   dried ancho chile peppers

1   dried New Mexico chile pepper

2   dried red chile peppers

    Sugar, to taste

1   (12-oz.) can beer

1   oz. unsweetened chocolate

4   cups water

1/2   cup masa harina

1/2   cup cold water

1. In a large Dutch oven or heavy pot, heat oil over medium heat. Brown meat. Add onions and cook until soft.

2. In a blender or food processor, blend cumin, garlic, ground chiles, Tabasco, salt, jalapeños and tomatoes. Set aside.

3. Prepare dried peppers by removing stems, seeds and deveining. Place prepared peppers in a small saucepan. Cover slightly with warm

Notes..
....
....
....

water. Bring to a boil, and reduce heat to simmer 12 to 15 minutes. Place peppers and tomato mixture in blender (reserve water). Blend until smooth, and add to meat and onions.

4. Add sugar, beer and chocolate to mixture; simmer uncovered, 2 hours, stirring occasionally. Add reserved water as necessary to keep chili soupy.

5. One half hour before serving, mix masa with 1/2 cup water to make a paste and add to chili. Stir briskly and thicken chili.

6. During last half hour of cooking, stir frequently to avoid sticking. Add salt, to taste, and reserved water to increase heat (if desired).

Makes 12 servings.

Notes..
....
....
....

⚞ Z-DIAMOND CHILI ⚟

3 mild dry red chile peppers
2 lbs. ground beef
2 lbs. ground pork
1 white onion, finely chopped
3 garlic cloves, finely chopped
1 cup or 4-oz. diced green chiles
1 (8-oz.) can tomato sauce
3 celery stalks, finely chopped
1 tablespoon ground cumin
1 tablespoon oregano
1 bay leaf
3 tablespoons mild chili powder
1/4 teaspoon white pepper
1/2 teaspoon black pepper
1 beef bouillon cube
1 teaspoon paprika
1/2 oz. unsweetened chocolate
3 tablespoons cornmeal
1 tablespoon all-purpose flour
1/4 cup water
   Salt, to taste

1. Soak dry red peppers in warm water, 30 to 45 minutes. When peppers are soft, remove and reserve about 1 cup soaking water. In a blender or food processor, grind until fine.

2. In a Dutch oven or a heavy pot, brown beef and pork; drain off excess fat.

3. To meat, add onion and garlic. Cook 4 to 6 minutes, stirring occasionally. Add green chiles, tomato sauce, celery, cumin, oregano,

Notes..
....
....
....

bay leaf, chili powder, white pepper, black pepper, bouillon, ground red chiles, paprika and reserved soaking water.

4. Bring mixture to a full boil. Reduce heat and cover. Simmer 1 hour. Stir occasionally.

5. Add chocolate and stir until melted. Cover and simmer an additional 1/2 hour.

6. In a cup, mix cornmeal and flour. Add 1/4 cup water to make a thin paste. Stir paste into chili mixture. Cook, stirring constantly, until slightly thickened.

7. Remove bay leaf before serving. Season with salt to taste and reserved chile water to increase heat (if desired).

Makes 6 servings.

Notes..
....
....
....

✥ VEGETARIAN CHILI ✥

---

1   (28-oz.) can tomatoes, crushed
2   medium onions, chopped
2   (15-oz.) cans pinto beans
2   medium zucchini, halved lengthwise, sliced (2-1/2 cups)
1   (15-oz.) can red kidney beans
1   tablespoon chili powder
1   (15-oz.) can garbanzo beans
1   teaspoon ground cumin
1   (12- to 14-oz.) can hominy
3/4 teaspoon garlic powder
1   (6-oz.) can tomato paste
1/2 teaspoon sugar
2   (4-oz.) cans diced green chiles
1-1/2 cups Monterey Jack cheese, shredded
    Salt, to taste
    Dairy sour cream
    Fresh cilantro, garnish

1. In a Dutch oven or heavy pot, combine all ingredients, except cheese.

2. Heat to boiling; reduce heat. Simmer, covered, 30 minutes.

3. Remove from heat and add cheese; stir until melted. Salt to taste. Serve with dairy sour cream and garnish with cilantro, if desired.

Makes 8 servings.

Notes..
....
....
....

❧ WEST OF THE PECOS ☙ CHILI

3	tablespoons vegetable oil
6	lbs. lean beef, cut in 1-inch cubes
1/2	cup chili powder
2	teaspoons salt
2	tablespoons ground oregano
1	tablespoon cayenne pepper
4	garlic cloves
8	cups beef stock or broth
1/2	cup masa harina or cornmeal
1/2	cup cold water

1. Heat oil in a large Dutch oven or heavy pot over medium heat.

2. Add beef, about 1 lb. at a time, and brown, stirring constantly. Remove each pound as it browns.

3. Return browned meat to pot. Add seasonings and beef stock or broth. Cover and simmer 1-1/2 to 2 hours. Skim off excess fat.

4. Combine masa harina or cornmeal with cold water and stir into chili. Simmer an additional 30 minutes.

Makes 6 servings.

> *The Pecos river traverses New Mexico from north to south. Many chile farms exist along its banks using its vital water. Judge Roy Bean, a scoundrel himself, once said he was "the only law west of the Pecos."*

Notes..
....
....
....

CHILI PLUS

This chapter shows just how useful that little bit of leftover chili can be. Here I show you a variety of ways to enhance dishes by using chili as an ingredient. While each recipe includes a suggestion for a certain type of chili, feel free to use whichever type you have on hand. This can also be a favorite canned chili as well as homemade. Experiment a bit and you'll soon find new favorite combinations. In Chili Steak, I perk up everyday round steak with a lively addition of chili, bell peppers and a subtle coffee flavor.

Poached eggs never tasted as good as when they're prepared in my easy-to-fix Chili and Eggs. This particular dish makes a fine supper.

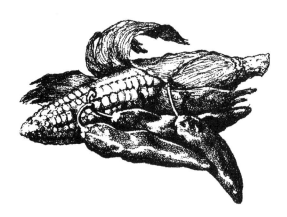

❧ CHILI CASSEROLE ❧ WITH POTATO

---

1 tablespoon vegetable oil
1 lb. coarsely ground pork or beef
1 chopped onion
2 cups Vegetarian Chili, page 114
1 cup cooked pinto beans
1 potato, peeled, thickly sliced
3 tomatoes, sliced

1. Preheat oven to 350F(175C). Spread oil in bottom of a 2-quart casserole dish.

2. In a skillet, brown meat. Layer meat, onion, chili, beans, potato and tomato slices in prepared casserole. Repeat layers until all ingredients are used.

3. Bake uncovered in preheated oven 1-1/2 hours.

Makes 6 servings.

Twenty-six miles northeast of Santa Fe is the Santuario de Chimayo. This famous healing shrine at El Potrero has been the destination of pilgrims since prehistoric times. First Native Americans, then Hispanos and later Anglos have traveled here seeking health and renewal. Today it continues to attract pilgrims, especially on Good Friday.

Notes..
....
....
....

❦ CHILI STEAK ❦

3 lbs. round steak, 1-inch thick
1 teaspoon salt
1/2 teaspoon black pepper
2 garlic cloves, crushed
3 tablespoons vegetable oil
1/2 cup chopped green peppers
1/2 cup chopped onion
1-1/2 cups Vegetarian Chili, page 114
1/2 cup strong black coffee

1. Cut steak into 6 serving pieces.

2. Mix salt, pepper and crushed garlic. Pat into both sides of steak; let stand in glass dish about 1 hour.

3. Pat steaks dry.

4. Heat oil in a large skillet over medium heat; brown steaks on both sides.

5. Remove steaks from skillet and set aside.

6. Cook green pepper and onion in skillet until soft. Add chili and coffee.

7. Return steaks to skillet and bring to a boil.

8. Reduce temperature; cover and cook 45 minutes. Serve over cooked rice.

Makes 6 servings.

Notes..
....
....
....

⊰ BAKED CHILI-TAMALES ⊱

1/3 cup lard or shortening
1 teaspoon salt
1/2 teaspoon baking powder
2 cups masa harina, or cornmeal
1-1/2 cups chicken broth
2 cups Vegetarian Chili, page 114, or Sweet Chili, page 109
1 cup shredded Longhorn cheese

1. Preheat oven to 350F(175C). Grease a 13 x 9-inch pan.

2. In a medium bowl, beat lard or shortening until light and creamy.

3. In a small bowl, combine salt, baking powder and masa harina or cornmeal. Beat into lard, a small amount at a time. Beat in chicken broth to make a soft light dough.

4. Spread 1/2 of dough in bottom of prepared pan. Spoon chili over dough.

5. Spread remaining dough over the chili.

6. Bake in preheated oven about 45 minutes.

7. Cut into 8 tamales. Sprinkle with shredded cheese and serve immediately.

Makes 8 tamales.

Notes..
....
....
....

❧ CHILI TOSTADAS ❧

Peanut or vegetable oil
8   tortillas
2   cups refried beans
1   cup Cowpoke Chili, page 101, or Gringo Chili, page 103
1   cup shredded lettuce
1   cup Guacamole, below
1   tomato, chopped

1. Heat 1/2-inch peanut or vegetable oil in a skillet and fry tortillas on both sides until crisp.

2. Spread 1/4 cup refried beans evenly on top of each tortilla; top with 2 tablespoons of heated chili.

3. Spread shredded lettuce on top, and spoon on 1/4 cup guacamole. Sprinkle with chopped tomatoes.

Makes 4 servings.

GUACAMOLE
3   ripe avocados, peeled, pitted
1   tablespoon chopped onion
1   tomato, chopped fine
1/2   teaspoon garlic salt
1   tablespoon lemon juice
12   drops Tabasco pepper sauce, optional

In a medium-size bowl, mash the avocados. Add remaining ingredients and mix well.

Notes...
....
....
....

❧{ RED-EYE HOMINY }❧

2 cups Mesilla Valley Chili, page 105
2 (15-oz.) cans hominy, rinsed, drained
1-1/2 cups shredded cheddar cheese
1 cup jalapeño peppers, seeded, deveined, diced

1. Preheat oven to 350F(175C). Butter a 2-quart casserole. Combine chili and hominy and place in prepared casserole.

2. Sprinkle 1/2 cup cheese over hominy mixture and stir in.

3. Spoon 1/2 cup cheese over mixture and top with jalapeño peppers.

4. Place in oven. Cover and bake in preheated oven 35 minutes.

5. Remove cover and sprinkle remaining cheese over top.

6. Return to oven and bake uncovered 10 more minutes.

Makes 6 servings.

> *ANASAZI (the Ancient Ones)—were the first to live in New Mexico. The ruins of their towns, each contained in one large, crescent-shape, multistory enclave, indicated a very advanced civilization. They are said to have wandered across the Bering Strait from Asia many thousands of years ago. Around A.D. 1200, they migrated to the Rio Grande and other scattered sites where the Spaniards found their pueblos in the 16th Century.*

Notes...
....
....
....

❧ STUFFED ON THE PECOS ☙

3 lbs. lean ground beef
2 tablespoons onion salt
1-1/2 cups Vegetarian Chili, page 114, or Jose's Fast Chili, page 104
6 tablespoons shredded Cheddar cheese
1 cup cooked black beans or pinto beans, drained

1. Mix ground beef and onion salt in a medium bowl.

2. Divide beef into 12 equal balls; flatten each ball into a 5-inch patty.

3. Spoon 1/4 cup chili on center of each patty.

4. Spoon 1/6 of beans on top of chili.

5. Sprinkle 1 tablespoon of shredded cheese over chili and beans.

6. Place a patty over chili and cheese. Press edges together. Repeat with remaining patties.

7. Heat a large skillet or broiler. Place patties in skillet and cook well on both sides, or broil both sides until cooked through, about 14 minutes. For grilling, wrap patties in foil.

Makes 6 servings.

We like to serve these stuffed burgers garnished with chopped green bell peppers and chopped black olives.

Notes..
....
....
....

❧ CHILI & EGGS ❧

2 cups Vegetarian Chili, page 114, or Chili Colorado, page 100
8 eggs, fried or poached
4 double-thick slices bread
   Butter or margarine

1. In a small saucepan, heat chili over medium heat.

2. Cook eggs as you like them. Keep warm.

3. Spread both sides of bread slices with butter. Fry on both sides until golden or broil both sides.

4. Spoon chili over toast and top with 2 eggs on each slice.

Makes 4 servings.

> *In some parts of the country, double-thick slices of bread are called Texas Toast.*

Notes...
....
....
....

ᵈᵉᶠ{ TRAIL-BOSS }ᵉᶠ TORTILLAS

Peanut or vegetable oil
4   large flour tortillas
2   cups Sweet Chili, page 109, or Rio Grande Red, page 108
8   slices Monterey Jack cheese
4   teaspoons pickled jalapeño peppers
1   onion, thinly sliced

1. Heat about 1 inch of peanut or vegetable oil in a skillet. Dip tortillas in hot oil a few seconds to soften.

2. Remove and place 1/2 cup chili in the center of each tortilla.

3. Fold in half, holding tortilla closed with tongs, and return to hot oil. Fry until crisp. Turn once.

4. Remove from oil and drain on paper towel.

5. Place two tortillas on each plate, top with a piece of cheese.

6. Put plate on top rack of oven and broil to melt the cheese.

7. Serve topped with jalapeño peppers and onion.

Makes 4 servings.

In New Mexico, there is an unwritten law that no cowboy can ride his horse on the windward side of the chuckwagon fire in a cow camp. The rule is observed so no trash or dirt will be stirred up and blown into the kettles or skillets. The chuckwagon cook (known as Cosi*) will run off any green hand who violates this serious breach of manners.*

Notes..
....
....
....

SAUCES

The heart—some say the soul—of New Mexico cooking is its sauces. I'm sure I could write a book on the infinite variety of sauces that are prepared in the Land of Enchantment. While I have given you a few choice ones, you may be pleasantly surprised to see just how much they vary. Everything from mild to hot is included, along with the basics that you can embellish as you choose.

Chipotle Chile Sauce is one I recommend you try. It has a distinctive smokey flavor not found in any other chile. These unusual chiles can be purchased either dried or canned. When using the canned chiles, be sure to drain them well before adding them to a dish.

My Hot Citrus Barbecue Sauce gives a lively flavor to chicken as well as pork and beef. Try it for your next barbecue and see the smiles of approval.

❧ ALMOND RED SAUCE ☙

1/2 cup toasted, slivered almonds
2 tablespoons vegetable oil
1 cup finely chopped onion
1 garlic clove, crushed
2 teaspoons paprika
1 teaspoon ground red chiles
1/4 teaspoon ground chili powder

1. Place almonds in a food processor or in blender; cover and process until finely ground.

2. In a small skillet, heat oil over medium heat. Add onion and garlic; stir frequently until onion is tender.

3. Stir in remaining ingredients, except almonds. Heat to boiling; reduce heat. Simmer 1 minute, stirring constantly. Stir in almonds. Serve hot. This full-bodied sauce is especially good with beef or pork.

Makes about 1-3/4 cups.

Green chile—In southern New Mexico, mature, high-quality chile is ready for the market in mid- or late July. Fresh chile remains on market counters until the first frost.

Red chile—The season for fresh red chile is naturally shorter than for the green. Some chile farmers market their entire crop as fresh ripe chile, but many market part of the crop green and the remainder as red.

Notes...
....
....
....

⊰{ ANCHO MOLE SAUCE }⊱

2 New Mexican dried chiles, seeded, stems removed
2 ancho dried chiles, seeded, stems removed
1 small onion, chopped
1 garlic clove, chopped
1 medium tomato, peeled, seeded, chopped
1/4 cup almonds, blanched
1/4 cup corn tortillas, cut into pieces
1/8 teaspoon ground coriander
1/8 teaspoon ground cloves
1/8 teaspoon ground cinnamon
1/4 cup raisins
1-1/2 tablespoons vegetable oil
1/2 cup chicken broth
1 oz. bitter chocolate

1. Combine all ingredients, except vegetable oil, chicken broth and chocolate; purée until mixture is smooth.

2. Heat oil in skillet and sauté the purée about 10 minutes, stirring frequently. Add broth and chocolate. Cook until sauce thickens.

Makes about 1 cup.

> *Want to join the Chili Appreciation Society?*
> *Write Chili Appreciation Society International*
> *c/o Frank X. Tolbert, Tolbert's Original Chili*
> *Parlor, 3802 Cedar Springs, Dallas, TX 75219.*

Notes..
....
....
....

❧ BASIC GREEN SAUCE ❧

1/2 cup vegetable oil
  1 cup chopped onions
 10 oz. fresh spinach, chopped
  2 garlic cloves, crushed
1/2 lb. tomatillos, coarsely chopped
  1 (4-oz.) can chopped green chiles
  1 tablespoon dried-leaf oregano
  1 cup chicken broth
  2 cups dairy sour cream

1. In a 3-quart saucepan, heat oil; cook and stir onions until tender.

2. Stir in remaining ingredients, except broth and dairy sour cream.

3. Cover and cook over medium heat 5 minutes, stirring occasionally.

4. Place mixture in a food processor or blender and process until smooth.

5. Return to saucepan; stir in broth. Bring to a boil, reduce heat. Simmer uncovered 10 minutes.

6. Stir in dairy sour cream. Cover and refrigerate up to 1 week; freeze for longer storage. Reheat before using.

Makes about 4 cups.

Notes...
....
....
....

❧ BASIC RED SAUCE ❧

8   dried ancho chiles
3-1/2   cups warm water
1/4   cup vegetable oil
1/2   cup chopped onion
2   garlic cloves, chopped
1   tablespoon dried-leaf oregano
1   tablespoon cumin seeds
1   teaspoon salt

1. In a bowl, cover chiles with warm water. Let stand about 30 minutes, until softened.

2. Strain chiles and reserve liquid. Remove stems, seeds and devein. Set aside.

3. Heat oil in a 2-quart saucepan. Add onion and garlic; stir until onion is tender. Stir in chiles, 2 cups reserved liquid and the remaining ingredients.

4. Heat to boiling; reduce heat. Simmer uncovered 20 minutes; cool.

5. Pour into a food processor or into a blender; cover and purée. Rub purée through a fine strainer and discard residue. Cover and refrigerate up to 10 days.

Makes 2-1/2 cups.

Notes..
....
....
....

✦{ CHIPOTLE CHILE SAUCE }✦

2   dried chipotle chiles
2   slices bacon, diced
1/4 cup finely chopped onion
1   cup beef broth
3   cups finely chopped tomatoes
1/4 cup finely chopped carrot
1/4 cup finely chopped celery
1/4 cup chopped fresh cilantro
1/4 teaspoon black pepper
1/2 teaspoon salt

1. Cover chiles with warm water. Let stand about 1 hour, until softened. Drain and finely chop.

2. In a 2-quart saucepan, cook and stir bacon and onion, until bacon is crisp; stir in chiles and remaining ingredients. Cook until vegetables are tender.

Makes about 4 cups.

Chipotle is the name of the smoked and dried red jalapeño chile pepper. Because its flavor is concentrated, it is hotter than the fresh jalapeño. Make this sauce as hot as you want by adding up to a total of 4 dried chipotle chiles.

Notes...
....
....
....

ENCHILADA SAUCE

2   tablespoons butter
2   garlic cloves
6   tablespoons mild chili powder
1   (14-1/2-oz.) can plum tomatoes
2   tablespoons tomato paste
1   cup chicken stock
1   cup water
1/4   teaspoon salt
1/8   teaspoon black pepper
1/2   cup fresh cilantro, finely minced

1. In a 1-1/2 or 2-quart saucepan, heat butter; add garlic and sauté 1 to 2 minutes.

2. Reduce heat to low and stir in chili powder. Cook, stirring constantly, 2 to 3 minutes to remove raw chile taste. Watch carefully because chili powder burns easily. Remove from heat.

3. Mash tomatoes with fork. Add tomatoes, tomato paste, chicken stock and water to saucepan. Reduce heat and simmer, stirring frequently, 10 minutes.

4. Taste and adjust salt and pepper to taste. Stir in cilantro after cooking is complete. Sauce may be used immediately or refrigerated 3 or 4 days. For longer storage, freeze sauce.

Makes about 2-1/2 cups.

Notes...
....
....
....

⊰{ HOT CHILE SAUCE }⊱

---

  4 cups water
 10 to 12 dried cascabel or jalapeño or pequín chile peppers
1/2 cup red-wine vinegar
  2 teaspoons dry mustard
  2 garlic cloves
1/2 cup olive or vegetable oil

1. In a large saucepan, heat water to boiling; stir in chiles.

2. Boil uncovered 5 minutes; drain and remove stems.

3. Place chiles, vinegar, mustard and garlic in a blender or food processor. Cover and blend until the chiles are finely chopped.

4. Gradually pour in oil, blending until smooth.

Makes about 1-1/2 cups.

New Mexico has over 10-million acres of public land managed by the Bureau of Land Management. Native American Indian reservations and pueblos occupy a significant historical portion of this Land of Enchantment.

Notes..
....
....
....

❧{ HOT CITRUS }❧ BARBECUE SAUCE

---

 1 tablespoon vegetable oil
 1 large onion, finely chopped
 1 tablespoon ground red chiles
1/4 teaspoon ground red pepper
 1 ancho chile, seeded, finely chopped
 1 cup orange juice
 2 tablespoons sugar
1/2 cup lime juice
 2 tablespoons lemon juice
 1 teaspoon salt
 2 tablespoons sugar
 1 tablespoon snipped fresh cilantro

1. In a skillet, heat oil; add onion, ground red chiles, red pepper and ancho chile. Stirring frequently, cook until onion is tender, about 5 minutes.

2. Stir in remaining ingredients. Heat to a rolling boil; reduce heat to low.

3. Simmer uncovered about 10 minutes. Stir occasionally.

Makes about 2-1/3 cups.

Notes..
....
....
....

❧ JALAPEÑO CREAM ❧ SAUCE

2   teaspoons vegetable oil
1   jalapeño pepper, seeded, finely chopped (use more
        or less, depending on how hot you want your sauce)
1   garlic clove, finely chopped
    Salt and black pepper, to taste
1   cup crème fraîche, recipe below

1. Heat oil in a small skillet. Add chile(s) and garlic; cook over low heat, stirring frequently until tender, about 4 minutes.

2. Remove from heat; stir in remaining ingredients, including crème fraîche.

Makes about 1-1/4 cups.

QUICK CRÈME FRAÎCHE
1/3   cup whipping cream
2/3   cup dairy sour cream
Gradually stir whipping cream into dairy sour cream until thoroughly blended. Cover and refrigerate up to 48 hours.

Notes..
....
....
....

⊰ NEW MEXICO ⊱ BARBECUE SAUCE

1	cup catsup
1/2	cup firmly packed brown sugar
1/4	cup lime juice
2	tablespoons ground red chiles
1	tablespoon vegetable oil
1	tablespoon Worchestershire sauce
2	jalapeño chile peppers, seeded, finely chopped
1-1/2	cups chopped onion
2	garlic cloves, finely chopped
1	(12-oz.) can beer
1	(12-oz.) can tomato paste

1. In a 2-quart saucepan, heat all ingredients to boiling; reduce heat to low.

2. Cover and simmer 1 hour, stirring occasionally.

3. Pour desired amount in a serving bowl. Place remainder in a container and refrigerate.

Makes about 5-1/2 cups.

New Mexico is the only state in the union that many Americans think is a foreign country. Even our license plates have USA on them. You do NOT need a passport to visit here.

Notes..
....
....
....

⊰{ NEW MEXICO }⊱ GREEN SAUCE

---

2 tablespoons vegetable oil
1 large onion, finely chopped
1 jalapeño chile, seeded, finely chopped
4 poblano chiles, roasted, peeled, seeded, finely chopped
   (about 1/2 cup)
1 garlic clove, finely chopped
1/2 cup whipping cream
1/4 teaspoon salt

1. In a skillet, heat oil and add onion, chiles and garlic. Cook over medium heat, stirring occasionally, until onion is tender, about 8 minutes.

2. Stir in whipping cream and salt.

Makes about 1-1/3 cups.

The "Blue Hole" is five minutes from downtown Santa Rosa. This deep natural artesian lake has become world-famous to scuba divers who come here to explore this unusual spot in northeast New Mexico.

Notes...
....
....
....

❧ GREEN CHILE ❧ CON QUESO

2 tablespoons butter
2 tablespoons finely chopped onion
1 garlic clove, minced
1 tomato, peeled, finely chopped
1/2 cup finely chopped, roasted, peeled, seeded green chile
1/2 cup evaporated milk
2 cups (8-oz.) grated Cheddar cheese
Tortilla chips

1. Melt butter in top part of a double boiler.

2. Add onion and garlic; sauté over medium heat.

3. Add tomato and green chile; mix well.

4. Remove from heat; add milk and cheese.

5. Place over hot water and cook, stirring constantly, until cheese is melted.

6. Cover and continue cooking over simmering water until desired thickness.

7. Cool slightly and serve with tortilla chips.

Makes about 2-1/2 cups.

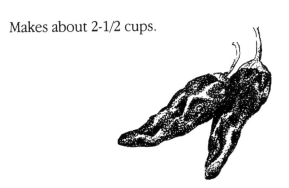

Notes . . . .
. . . .
. . . .
. . . .

SALSAS & RELISHES

In 1993, more salsa than ketchup was sold in the United States. Everyone has their favorite brand or their own version of a fresh or uncooked salsa. Don't believe the commercials that would have you think the best salsa is always made in Texas. New Mexico cafés were serving salsa long before it became the rage in other states.

Salsas and relishes add a refreshing combination of flavors that can enhance the most bland foods. They also add a delightful texture of their own. Serve them warm or chilled—the choice is yours. I have included Guacamole in this group because most times it is used in the same manner as a salsa or relish, accenting other foods. For those of you who are gardeners and have a surplus of zucchini, here is yet another way to enjoy them.

❧ CORN SALSA ❧

---

1   (16-oz.) can kernel corn, drained
1   (4-oz.) can chopped green chiles, drained
1   jalapeño chile, seeded, finely chopped
1/4   cup chopped green bell pepper
1/4   cup sliced green onions with tops
2   tablespoons white-wine vinegar
1   tablespoon vegetable oil
   Salt, to taste

1. In a serving bowl, mix all ingredients.

2. Cover and refrigerate until chilled, about 1 hour.

Makes about 2-1/3 cups.

From the time Don Juan de Oñate entered New Mexico in 1598, the building blocks of the state's history have been well-laced with chile. The Spaniards are said to have brought the vegetable north from the tropical area of the New World. There is, however, mounting evidence that the ancestors of the Pueblo Indians may have cultivated chiles prior to the Spanish colonization of the Southwest. It is clear that chiles played a role not unlike that of the black pepper in the Old World.

Notes...
....
....
....

❧ CUCUMBER SALSA ❧

---

2 medium cucumbers, peeled, seeded, coarsely shredded
1 cup dairy sour cream
1 cup plain yogurt
1/4 cup chopped fresh parsley
1/4 cup chopped fresh cilantro
1 teaspoon ground cumin
   Salt, to taste

1. In a serving bowl, mix all ingredients.

2. Serve at once or refrigerate until chilled.

Salsa may be stored, covered in refrigerator, about 2 hours.

Makes about 3 cups.

New Mexico covers an area of 121,000 square miles of diverse terrain. From top to bottom it plunges through six of the seven life zones, from the tundra to the Lower Sonoran Desert. The world-famous Rio Grande river runs the length of the state, north to south.

Notes...
....
....
....

❧ FRESH-TOMATO SALSA ❧

2   medium tomatoes, peeled, seeded
2   serrano chile peppers, peeled, seeded, deveined
2   yellow-wax chile peppers, peeled, seeded, deveined
3   radishes, trimmed
3   cloves garlic
1   bunch green onions, trimmed, or 1/2 medium onion
1   cup cilantro leaves
    Salt, to taste
1   tablespoon tomato paste
1/2   cup water

1. Coarsely chop the first seven ingredients. Pieces should be chunky, not minced. Place in a glass or plastic bowl.

2. In a cup, stir together salt, tomato paste and water. Mix well.

3. Pour over chopped ingredients and mix well. Serve at once or refrigerate until chilled. This salsa can be refrigerated up to one week.

Makes 6 servings.

Notes..
....
....
....

❧ TOMATILLO SALSA ❧

3	fresh or canned tomatillos
1/3	cup diced fresh pineapple
1/3	cup chopped red onion
1/4	cup diced red or green bell pepper
2	tablespoons chopped fresh cilantro
3	tablespoons fresh orange juice
1-1/2	tablespoons fresh lime juice
1	tablespoon white vinegar
1	garlic clove, minced
1-1/2	teaspoons jalapeño, chipotle or other chile
	Salt and black pepper, to taste

1. Remove husks from fresh tomatillos and finely chop. Color should be bright-green, not yellow when skinned. If you use canned tomatillos, purée in a food processor.

2. Combine all ingredients in a glass or plastic bowl. Cover and refrigerate until chilled.

3. Salsa may be stored, covered, 2 days in refrigerator.

Makes 4 servings.

Notes..
....
....
....

❈{ WINTER SALSA }❈

1	cup chopped, peeled, seeded cucumber
1-1/2	cups chopped, seeded tomato
1	cup chopped, seeded red bell pepper
1/2	cup chopped radishes
1/2	cup chopped red onion
3	tablespoons minced shallots
1/4	cup minced cilantro
1	teaspoon chopped, canned jalapeño pepper
	Salt, to taste
1	tablespoon lime juice
3	tablespoons fresh orange juice

1. Combine all ingredients in a glass or plastic bowl. The acid could react to a metal bowl, giving the salsa a bad taste.

2. Marinate at room temperature at least 1 hour.

Makes 4 to 6 servings.

> *When one of my recipes calls for fresh chiles and none are available, commercially frozen chiles are the next-best thing. I suggest you use the New Mexico green chiles that are available in many supermarket frozen-food departments.*

Notes...
....
....
....

❧ GUACAMOLE ❧

---

1   large ripe avocado, peeled, pitted
1   medium tomato
1   small onion
1   small green bell pepper
1   (4-oz.) can chopped green chiles
1-2   tablespoons lemon juice
    Salt to taste

1. Chop all ingredients finely. Do not mash.

2. In a serving dish, mix all ingredients together with lemon juice and salt to taste.

Makes about 2-1/2 cups.

VARIATION: We add a teaspoon of jalapeño juice and use as a sandwich filling. Serve with corn chips on the side.

Serve as a dip or as a salad with lettuce and corn chips. Essentially guacamole is a blend of avocados, onion, garlic and lemon juice. There are as many recipes as there are cooks here in New Mexico. Some like to purée the avocado. Try various mixtures and consistencies until you find one that suits you.

Notes...
....
....
....

❧ RADISH & CILANTRO ❧ RELISH

2	cups thinly sliced radishes
1/2	cup chopped onion
2	tablespoons lime juice
2	tablespoons oil
3	tablespoons orange juice
2	tablespoons chopped fresh cilantro
1/8	teaspoon freshly ground black pepper
	Salt, to taste

1. Mix all ingredients in a glass or plastic bowl.

2. Cover and refrigerate at least 1 hour.

Makes about 3 cups.

The Margarita, a drink based on tequila and lime juice (and often Triple Sec, too), is one of the most popular with New Mexico chili lovers. However, at chili cookoffs, beer and wine are also in demand.

Notes...
....
....
....

⋈ SOUTHWEST RELISH ⋊

---

 1   cup chopped, fresh tomatillos, husks removed
3/4 cup chopped, seeded tomato
3/4 cup diced, seeded yellow bell pepper
3/4 cup diced, seeded green bell pepper
 2   garlic cloves, finely chopped
1/4 cup (1-oz.) pine nuts, toasted
 2   tablespoons lemon juice
 1   tablespoon snipped, fresh sage leaves
     Salt, to taste

1. Mix all ingredients in a glass or plastic bowl.

2. Cover and refrigerate at least 1 hour.

Makes about 3-3/4 cups.

The city of Albuquerque was founded in 1706 by Father Manuel Moreno. He is said to have walked with a band of followers from Santa Fe, a distance of more than 60 miles, to what is known today as "Old Town" in Albuquerque.

Notes..
....
....
....

⋅ঙ{ ZUCCHINI RELISH }ঌ⋅

```
   2  cups shredded zucchini
   2  tablespoons oil
 1/4  cup fresh snipped cilantro
 1/4  teaspoon sugar
   2  tablespoons lime juice
   1  tablespoon salt
 1/4  teaspoon black pepper
```

1. Mix all ingredients in a glass or plastic bowl.

2. Cover and refrigerate at least 1 hour before serving.

Makes about 2-1/2 cups.

> *The Rio Grande river runs from Colorado to the Texas-Mexican border through the center of New Mexico. It rushes through narrow gorges in the north then lazily wanders out into the fertile valleys of the south. The Rio Grande is a prime source of water. Six other rivers in the Land of Enchantment are also important to its economy: the Pecos, Canadian, Chama, San Juan, Brazos and Gila.*

Notes...

CAKES & DESSERTS

A mulberry tree at my grandparents homestead ranch is one of my fondest memories. I used to eat mulberries until I was both blue and ill. When I moved to Roswell, New Mexico, I found a number of mulberry trees and, best of all, a great recipe for Maple Mulberry Cake. Try it and you'll be pleasantly surprised. If you can't find mulberries, use blueberries, which make an excellent substitute.

Pecans are a major cash crop in New Mexico. We use pecans in many cakes because they add a special flavor that is gaining in popularity. Toasting them before using heightens their wonderful flavor. It is almost as common here in our dishes as it is in Southern cooking.

If you have ever eaten in a New Mexico restaurant, I'm sure you have enjoyed *sopaipillas,* so famous here in the Land of Enchantment. These puffy pillows of pleasure are easy to fix and the perfect ending to dinner. Served with warm honey, these little gems were the start of my love affair with this cuisine. I have included the best recipe I've found in many years of study and experimentation—a must if you want to serve an authentic New Mexican meal.

You are in for a treat the first time you sample *Capirotada.* This version of Mexican bread pudding is worth a little effort. It is delightfully sweet with wine-soaked raisins. Your family or guests will reward you with compliments when you serve them this dish.

❧ FRESH APPLE CAKE ❧

3 cups all-purpose flour
1 tablespoon baking powder
1/4 teaspoon salt
1 teaspoon baking soda
1 tablespoon ground cinnamon
3 eggs
2 cups sugar
1 cup vegetable oil
2 teaspoons vanilla extract
4 apples, unpeeled, cored, grated
1 cup pecans

1. Preheat oven to 350F(175C). Generously grease a 10-inch tube or Bundt pan with shortening and flour.

2. In a medium-size bowl, sift together flour, baking powder, salt, soda and cinnamon. Set aside.

3. In a large bowl, beat eggs; add sugar and beat well. Add oil and vanilla extract; beat well.

4. Add apples to batter. Stir well. Stir in pecans and pour into prepared cake pan. Bake about 1 hour or until top springs back.

5. Immediately turn out of pan. This very moist cake keeps well.

Makes 8 to 10 servings.

Notes..
....
....
....

❧{ PUMPKIN LOAF }❧

1	cup packed brown sugar
1/2	cup granulated sugar
1	cup cooked or canned pumpkin
1/2	cup vegetable oil
2	eggs
2	cups all-purpose flour
1	teaspoon baking soda
1/2	teaspoon grated nutmeg
1/2	teaspoon ground cinnamon
1/4	teaspoon ground ginger
1	cup raisins
1/2	cup chopped pecans
1/4	cup water

1. Preheat oven to 350F(175C); grease and flour a 9 x 5-inch loaf pan.

2. Place sugars, pumpkin, oil, and eggs in a large bowl; beat well. Sift in flour, soda, nutmeg, cinnamon and ginger; stir in. Add raisins, pecans, water, and mix well.

3. Spoon into prepared pan and bake 1-1/4 to 1-1/2 hours or until done. Cool on wire rack.

4. Let set overnight and slice. Cake is better after 24 hours.

Makes 8 servings.

Notes...
....
....
....

❧ MAPLE MULBERRY CAKE ❧

1/4　cup shortening
1/2　cup maple syrup
1/2　cup packed brown sugar
3/4　cup dairy sour cream
　2　eggs, beaten
　1　cup ripe mulberries or blueberries
　2　cups all-purpose flour
　1　teaspoon ground ginger
　1　teaspoon baking powder
1/4　teaspoon salt
1/2　cup mulberry juice
　　　Lemon Glaze, recipe below

1. Preheat oven to 350F(175C). Generously grease a 10-inch springform tube pan. Heat shortening, syrup and sugar in a saucepan over medium heat. Remove from heat. Set aside.

2. Add dairy sour cream, beaten eggs and mulberries.

3. In a small bowl, sift together dry ingredients and add to batter. Mix well and pour into prepared pan.

4. Bake about 30 minutes, or until knife inserted comes out dry.

5. After cake cools, pour reserved mulberry juice over cake to moisten before applying Lemon Glaze.

Makes 10 servings.

LEMON GLAZE
　1　tablespoon milk
　2　tablespoons lemon juice
3/4　cup confectioners' sugar

In a small bowl, gradually blend milk and lemon juice into confectioners' sugar and pour over cake.

Notes..
....
....
....

❧{ PUMPKIN-PECAN CAKE }❧

```
1/2   cup shortening
1-1/2 cups sugar
  3   eggs
  1   cup cooked or canned pumpkin
2/3   cup milk
1-3/4 cups all-purpose flour
1/2   cup dry powdered milk
  2   teaspoons baking powder
  1   teaspoon baking soda
  1   teaspoon salt
  2   teaspoons ground cinnamon
1/4   teaspoon ground allspice
1/2   teaspoon grated nutmeg
1/4   teaspoon ground ginger
  1   cup coarsely chopped pecans
      Lemon Glaze, page 151
```

1. Preheat oven to 350F(175C). Lightly grease and flour a 13 x 9-inch pan. In a large bowl, cream shortening and sugar until fluffy. Beat eggs in one at a time.

2. In a small bowl, combine pumpkin and milk and add to shortening mixture.

3. In a small bowl, sift all dry ingredients together and add to the pumpkin mixture.

4. Beat well; add nuts. Turn into prepared pan.

5. Bake about 40 to 45 minutes.

6. Cool on rack. Frost with Lemon Glaze.

Makes 10 to 12 servings.

Notes...
....
....
....

❧ TOASTED ❧ PECAN-COCONUT CAKE

6   tablespoons butter, softened to room temperature
1   cup finely chopped pecans
2   cups shredded sweetened coconut
1   yellow cake mix plus required ingredients specified on mix
1   (8 oz.) pkg. cream cheese, softened
2   teaspoons milk
3   cups confectioners' sugar
1   teaspoon vanilla extract

1. Preheat oven according to directions on cake mix box. Generously grease 3 (8-inch) baking pans. Melt 3 tablespoons butter in a skillet over medium heat. Allow the remaining butter to soften to room temperature.

2. Add pecans and coconut to skillet and stir constantly until mixture is golden brown. Remove from skillet and drain on paper towels.

3. Mix cake according to directions on box. Add one cup of toasted pecan-coconut mixture. Divide batter among prepared pans and bake as directed on the box. Remove from oven and cool.

4. To make frosting, cream remaining butter with cream cheese until light and fluffy. Stir in milk and vanilla. Add sugar one cup at a time, beating well until mixture reaches spreading consistency.

5. Reserve 1/2 cup toasted mixture to sprinkle on top. Add remaining mixture to frosting. Frost cake and sprinkle with reserved toasted mixture.

Makes 10 servings.

Notes..
....
....
....

❦ ZUCCHINI PINEAPPLE ❧ CAKE

3   eggs
2   cups sugar
2   tablespoons vanilla extract
1   cup oil
2   cups grated, peeled zucchini
3   cups all-purpose flour
1   teaspoon baking powder
1   teaspoon salt
1   teaspoon baking soda
1   teaspoon ground cinnamon
1   cup chopped pecans
1   cup crushed pineapple, drained
    Cream Cheese Frosting, page 155

1. Preheat oven to 325F(160C). Generously grease 2 (8-inch) cake pans.

2. In a large bowl, beat eggs until fluffy; add sugar, vanilla extract, oil and zucchini; mix well.

3. In a medium-size bowl, mix dry ingredients and stir into egg mixture. Add pecans and pineapple to egg mixture.

4. Pour batter into prepared pan and bake 1 hour.

Makes 10 servings.

Notes...
....
....
....

CREAM CHEESE FROSTING

1   lb. confectioners' sugar
2   teaspoons vanilla extract
1   (8-oz.) pkg. cream cheese, softened
1   cup butter, softened
1/2   cup chopped pecans
1/4   cup shredded coconut
    Dash of salt

1. In a medium-size bowl, thoroughly combine all ingredients except pecans and coconut.

2. Frost and decorate top with pecans and coconut.

Yields frosting for 2 (8-inch) layers, top and sides.

Abundant harvests of pecans inspire us to include this sweet nut in many of our tasty desserts.

Notes..
....
....
....

⊰{ BISCUIT PUDDING }⊱

---

3   cups biscuit or soft bread crumbs
2   tablespoons butter
1/8 teaspoon ground cloves
1   cup packed brown sugar
1   cup water
1/4 teaspoon ground cinnamon
1   cup (4 oz.) shredded Cheddar cheese
1   cup dried apple slices
1/2 cup raisins
1/2 cup chopped pecans
1/2 cup softened butter
     Sweetened whipped cream

1. Preheat oven to 300F(145C). Spread crumbs in a shallow baking pan and lightly dot with 2 tablespoons butter. Bake in preheated oven until golden brown.

2. In a small saucepan, combine cloves, brown sugar, water and ground cinnamon over medium heat, stirring constantly until sugar dissolves and becomes syrup.

3. In a 9-inch ungreased casserole dish, spread 1 cup of crumbs. Pour 1/3 cup of syrup over crumbs and sprinkle with cheese.

4. Top with another cup of crumbs and sprinkle on the apples, raisins and pecans.

5. Top with 1/3 cup of syrup and balance of crumbs; pour balance of syrup over the mixture.

6. Dot with remaining butter. Bake uncovered in preheated oven 25 to 30 minutes or until mixture bubbles.

7. Cool at least 15 minutes before serving. Top with sweetened whipped cream.

Makes 6 servings.

Notes..
....
....
....

❧{ CINNAMON-HONEY }❧
BUTTER

1   cup butter
1/2   to 3/4 cup honey
1   teaspoon ground cinnamon

1. In a small bowl, cream butter; gradually beat in honey and ground cinnamon.

2. Cover and store in refrigerator.

3. Serve with Sopaipillas. Also excellent on toast or hot biscuits.

Makes about 8 (1-1/2 cup) servings.

Typical New Mexico homes are complex, spiritually oriented, and socially organized domains. Built according to long-standing tradition, whether tepee, adobe, pueblo, hogan, ranch house or bunkhouse, they are designed to protect access to their interior space. Most are square or rectangular, except for the tepees of the Apache or the hogans of the Navajo.

Notes..
....
....
....

❧ CAPIROTADA ❧

1/2	cup raisins
1	cup Madeira or sweet wine
12-14	slices day-old French bread
1/2	cup piñon nuts or pecans
2	cups sugar
3-1/2	cups water
1	teaspoon ground cinnamon
5	tablespoons butter
1-1/2	teaspoons vanilla extract
1	cup shredded Jack or Longhorn cheese (4 oz.)
	Whipped cream or ice cream

1. Place raisins in bowl and cover with Madeira; soak at least 20 minutes.

2. Preheat oven to 350F(175C). Butter a 13 x 9-inch baking dish.

3. Tear bread into bite-size pieces, place in a shallow baking pan. Toast in oven 10 minutes.

4. Remove bread from oven. In a mixing bowl, toss bread and piñon nuts.

5. Place sugar in a saucepan over medium-high heat, stirring constantly, until sugar melts and turns to light caramel color. Carefully add water and cinnamon, as the hot syrup may spatter as you add water. The caramel will partially solidify, but liquifies as it reheats.

6. Reduce heat and add butter, raisins and vanilla extract. Continue stirring until butter has melted.

Notes..
....
....
....

7. Pour bread mixture into prepared baking dish; mix in cheese. Pour syrup mixture over all.

8. Bake in preheated oven about 30 minutes.

9. Serve topped with whipped cream or ice cream.

Makes 6 to 8 servings.

This is the New Mexican version of bread pudding. It's delightfully sweet and the cheese is undetectable. Traditionally served during Lent, it's wonderful anytime.

Notes...
....
....
....

❧ NATILLAS ❧

4   eggs, separated
3/4   cup sugar
1/4   cup all-purpose flour
1/8   teaspoon salt
4   cups milk
1/2   teaspoon vanilla extract
    Ground cinnamon

1. In a medium-size bowl, beat egg yolks; stir in sugar, flour and salt. Thoroughly combine. Add 2 tablespoons milk and mix.

2. In a saucepan, bring remaining milk to simmer, or scald milk.

3. Stirring constantly, add egg yolks and sugar mixture. Reduce heat and simmer until the mixture is the consistency of thick custard.

4. Remove from heat and allow to cool; stir in vanilla extract.

5. In a large bowl, beat egg whites until they are stiff. Fold custard mixture into beaten egg whites.

6. Sprinkle with ground cinnamon and set aside 30 minutes. Serve warm or chilled.

Makes 4 servings.

Notes...
....
....
....

❧ PECAN PIE ❧

---

1 cup all-purpose unbleached flour
1/4 teaspoon salt
1/3 cup shortening
2 tablespoons cold water
1/4 cup sugar
2 tablespoons all-purpose flour
1/2 teaspoon salt
1 cup dark corn syrup
2 eggs, lightly beaten
1/2 cup evaporated milk
1 teaspoon vanilla extract
1 cup pecans

1. To make crust, mix flour and 1/4 teaspoon salt; using a pastry blender or 2 knives, cut in shortening until it resembles a coarse meal. Add water, sprinkling in enough to form a ball. Remove from mixing bowl and form it into a ball. Wrap in plastic wrap and refrigerate at least 20 minutes.

2. Preheat oven to 375F(190C). On a lightly floured surface, roll dough into a 10-inch circle. Pat and fit into a 9-inch pie plate; fold dough under the lip of the pie plate to form an edge; using your fingers, flute the top of the edge. Prick the dough with a fork; refrigerate while making the filling.

3. To make the filling, mix sugar, flour and salt. Mix in corn syrup. Add eggs, milk and vanilla; stir until smooth. Stir in pecans. Pour filling into the pie crust and bake in the center of the preheated oven 1 hour. Check after 40 minutes. If the top becomes too brown, cover with foil. Cool to room temperature before serving.

Makes 8 servings.

Notes..
....
....
....

❧ SOPAIPILLAS ❧

      2 cups unbleached flour
    1/2 teaspoon baking powder
    1/2 teaspoon salt
    1/2 teaspoon sugar
  1-1/2 teaspoons vegetable oil
      1 tablespoon evaporated milk
      2 tablespoons warm water
         Oil
         Honey

1. In a large mixing bowl, combine flour, baking powder, salt and sugar.

2. Add oil, evaporated milk and water; mix into a smooth dough.

3. On a floured surface, knead gently into a soft dough. The mixture will be slightly sticky. Let dough rest about 30 minutes.

4. Divide into 12 equal portions and roll into balls.

5. In a skillet or deep fryer, heat oil to 400F(205C). On a floured surface, roll each ball into a 10-inch circle, 1/4-inch thick. Cut each circle into 4 quarters and place in hot oil.

6. Carefully spoon oil over top of each sopaipilla; this causes it to start puffing. After 20 seconds, turn the sopaipillas over and brown the other side. Remove from oil with slotted spoon; drain on paper towels. Keep warm in 150F(135C) oven while cooking the balance.

Serve with honey or Pineapple Filling, page 163.

Makes 40 sopaipillas.

The traditional method of eating these delicious treats is to bite off one corner and pour honey inside. Also see recipe for Cinnamon Honey Butter, page 157.

Notes ....
....
....
....

❧ PINEAPPLE FILLING ❧

---

      2   tablespoons cornstarch
  2-1/2   tablespoons sugar
      1   (4-oz.) can crushed pineapple
          confectioners' sugar

1. In a small saucepan, combine cornstarch and sugar; stir in pineapple.

2. Cook mixture over medium heat, stirring until it boils. Stirring constantly, boil 1 minute. Cool slightly.

3. While sopaipillas are still hot, make a slit along one long side and one short side with sharp knife.

4. Gently lift top and fill with 1 tablespoon of warm filling.

5. Replace top and sprinkle with confectioners' sugar. Serve warm.

Makes about 1 cup.

Notes...
....
....
....

❧ SPANISH FRITTERS ❧

---

    1   cup sugar
    2   teaspoons ground cinnamon
    1   cup water
    2   tablespoons butter
    2   tablespoons vegetable shortening
    1   tablespoon sugar
  1/2   teaspoon salt
  1/2   cup white cornmeal
  1/2   cup all-purpose flour
    2   large eggs
        Oil for deep frying

1. In a small dish, combine 1 cup sugar and cinnamon; set aside. In a 3-quart saucepan, bring water, butter, shortening, sugar and salt to a full boil.

2. Remove from heat and briskly stir in cornmeal and flour.

3. Reduce heat to low; return pan to heat and stir vigorously until ball of dough is formed.

4. Remove from heat and immediately place dough in food processor. Add eggs. Process about 20 seconds, until smooth and shiny.

5. Heat 3 inches of oil in a deep, heavy skillet or deep fryer to 375F(190C).

6. Transfer dough to a pastry bag fitted with #5 Star tip. Pipe 8- to 10-inch strips of dough into hot oil. Fry on both sides until browned and crisp; be careful to keep oil a constant 375F(190C) for even cooking.

Notes..
....
....
....

7. Drain on paper towels; roll in sugar and cinnamon mixture to coat.

Makes 8 servings.

✛ **VARIATION**: Add 2 tablespoons of unsweetened cocoa and 2 tablespoons additional sugar with the eggs. Dust with confectioners' sugar.

✛ **VARIATION**: Add 1/2 teaspoon anise oil to the batter with the cornmeal and flour.

Notes..
....
....
....

COOKIES & CANDIES

I think my Pecan Fudge recipe is the best fudge I have ever eaten. Rich, creamy and easy to make, this is one you should try if none other. I traded a family recipe that I had never shared with anyone for this wonderful fudge. I have created a new recipe for Piñon Fudge with the same basic ingredients. I hope you'll find it as interesting as the Pecan Fudge.

No New Mexico Christmas is complete without *Biscochitos*. These jewels of the Southwest are the official cookie of New Mexico. Halfway between a shortbread and a sugar cookie, they are often baked in fancy shapes and are always enjoyed by young and old alike.

I've included one of my oldest recipes for Bunkhouse Cookies. This stick-to-your-ribs cookie was carried on horseback by cowboys and was regular fare on the cattle ranches here in New Mexico. I was raised on these hearty, old-style cookies. Although I use pecans in most of my cookies, many times I'll use peanuts, which are also raised here.

❧ BUNKHOUSE COOKIES ❧

---

      1   cup butter or margarine
    3/4   cup packed brown sugar
    3/4   cup granulated sugar
      2   eggs
  1-3/4   cups all-purpose flour
      2   cups uncooked oats
      2   teaspoons ground cinnamon
      1   teaspoon baking soda
    1/2   teaspoon salt, optional
      1   teaspoon sugar
      1   teaspoon ground cinnamon

1. Preheat oven to 375F(190C). Grease a baking sheet.

2. In a large bowl, beat together butter, brown sugar and 3/4 cup granulated sugar, until light and fluffy.

3. Add eggs and mix well.

4. In a medium-size bowl, combine flour, oats, 1 teaspoon ground cinnamon, baking soda and salt.

5. Add to sugar mixture and mix well.

6. Drop by rounded teaspoonful onto prepared baking sheet.

7. In a small bowl, combine remaining teaspoon sugar and 1 teaspoon cinnamon; sprinkle lightly over each cookie.

8. Bake 8 to 10 minutes. Cool 1 minute before removing to cooling rack.

Makes about 72 cookies.

Notes..
....
....
....

❧ BISCOCHITOS ❧

6 cups unbleached all-purpose flour, sifted
1 teaspoon baking powder
1 teaspoon salt
1 lb. butter, softened
1-1/2 cups sugar
2 teaspoons anise seeds
2 eggs
1/2 cup brandy
1/2 cup sugar
3 teaspoons ground cinnamon

1. Preheat oven to 350F(175C).

2. In a large bowl, combine flour with baking powder and salt. Sift again.

3. In another bowl, cream butter and 1-1/2 cups sugar. Add anise seeds; continue beating until light and fluffy.

4. In another bowl, beat eggs at high speed 2 minutes. Combine eggs and butter mixture.

5. Add flour mixture, 1 cup at a time, mixing well after each addition.

Notes..
....
....
....

6. Pour brandy over the dough and mix well.

7. On a lightly floured surface, roll dough to 1/4 inch thick; cut into desired shapes. In a small bowl, combine sugar and cinnamon. Dip each in sugar and cinnamon; place on a baking sheet. Bake in preheated oven 10 to 12 minutes until golden brown. Remove from oven. Sprinkle with additional sugar and cinnamon.

Makes about 72 cookies.

VARIATION: My friend Nellie Fields of Roswell substitutes whole cloves for anise seeds. She uses 3 eggs and 2 cups vegetable oil in place of the butter. The result is excellent.

Biscochitos are the official cookie of New Mexico. The unique rich anise flavor is the children's favorite. They are cut into various shapes for Christmas. No other holiday dish is as typical of New Mexico cuisine.

Notes...
....
....
....

❧ HONEY-NUT COOKIES ❧

---

  1   cup butter
  1   cup honey
  1   cup sugar
  1   egg
  3   cups all-purpose flour
  2   teaspoons baking powder
  2   teaspoons ground ginger
1/2   teaspoon vanilla extract
1-1/2   cups coarsely chopped peanuts or pecans

1. Preheat oven to 375F(190C). Grease baking sheets.

2. In a large bowl, cream butter; beat in honey, sugar and egg.

3. Stir in flour, baking powder and ground ginger; mix thoroughly. Stir in vanilla extract and nuts.

4. Drop by teaspoonful onto prepared baking sheets; and bake about 10 to 12 minutes.

Makes about 75 cookies.

Notes..
....
....
....

❧ MEXICAN WEDDING ❧ COOKIES

3/4	cup pecans
2	cups all-purpose flour
1/2	cup confectioners' sugar
1	cup butter, slightly softened
1	teaspoon vanilla extract
1/2	teaspoon almond extract
1	cup confectioners' sugar

1. Place pecans in food processor with 1 cup of the flour. Using pulsing method, grind together until nuts are fine.

2. In a medium-size bowl, beat 1/2 cup confectioners' sugar with butter. If butter is too soft, the cookie dough will be difficult to work. Stir in vanilla and almond extracts.

3. Add the nut-flour mixture to the butter. Beat in remaining cup of flour. Refrigerate the cookie dough 20 minutes.

4. Preheat oven to 350F(175C).

5. Shape dough into walnut-size balls and place on ungreased baking sheets.

6. Bake in preheated oven 10 to 12 minutes. Remove cookies to a cooling rack.

7. When cookies have cooled about 15 minutes, roll in confectioners' sugar to completely coat.

Makes about 32 cookies.

Notes...
....
....
....

❧ PECAN DROPS ❧

1   cup firmly packed brown sugar
1/3 cup evaporated milk
2   tablespoons corn syrup
6   oz. semi-sweet chocolate chips
1/2 cup chopped pecans
1   teaspoon vanilla extract
36   pecan halves

1. Combine brown sugar, evaporated milk and corn syrup in a heavy saucepan.

2. Bring to a boil over medium heat, stirring constantly, and boil 2 minutes. Remove from heat. Add chocolate chips, chopped pecans and vanilla extract; stir until chocolate is melted and mixture is slightly thickened.

3. Drop by rounded teaspoons onto waxed paper-lined baking sheets. Press pecan halves on top. Chill until firm, about 30 minutes.

Makes approximately 36 candies.

ZUNI PUEBLO, the largest of New Mexico's pueblos, is located 38 miles south of Gallup on NM 32. Zuni artisans are best known for their magnificent, detailed jewelry and pottery.

Notes...
....
....
....

❧{ PECAN FUDGE }❧

4-1/2 cups sugar
   1 cup evaporated milk
  15 oz. plain Hershey® candy bars, broken into small pieces
   1 (12-oz.) pkg. semi-sweet chocolate chips
   1 (7-oz.) jar marshmallow creme
1-1/2 teaspoons salt
   1 teaspoon vanilla extract
   2 cups chopped pecans
 1/4 cup margarine

1. Combine sugar and evaporated milk in a heavy 2-1/2-qt. saucepan. Over medium heat, bring to a full rolling boil, stirring constantly.

2. Continue boiling 5 minutes over medium heat, or until candy thermometer reaches 234F(110C), stirring constantly to prevent scorching.

3. Place Hershey® candy pieces, chocolate chips, marshmallow creme, salt and vanilla extract in a large mixing bowl.

4. Pour hot sugar mixture over chocolate, one half at a time. Mix thoroughly after each pour.

5. Add pecans and margarine and mix well.

6. Pour into a buttered 8-inch-square pan; let cool and cut into squares.

Makes about 5 lbs.

Notes..
....
....
....

❧ PIÑON BRITTLE ❧

---

  2   teaspoons butter
  2   cups sugar
  1   cup white corn syrup
1/2   cup water
  1   tablespoon butter
  2   cups raw piñon nuts
  1   teaspoon vanilla extract
  2   teaspoons baking soda

1. Using 2 teaspoons butter, coat 1 large or 2 small baking sheets.

2. In a large saucepan, combine sugar, syrup and water. Cook, stirring occasionally, until it reaches a soft ball stage, or about 234F(110C) on a candy thermometer.

3. Add 1 tablespoon butter and nuts; continue cooking and stirring until it is at a hard-crack stage, or 300F(150C); syrup will turn a pale caramel color.

4. Quickly remove from heat; add vanilla extract and soda. Stir rapidly to dissolve and mix well. Immediately pour as thinly as possible onto prepared sheets. Cool slightly and lift up with knife and pull up as thinly as possible.

Makes 6 servings.

Piñon nuts are the largest uncultivated crop in North America. They are harvested the second year after flowering. Because they are totally dependent on rainfall, they are not always available. The last bumper crop in New Mexico was in 1976 when over 4-million pounds were harvested.

Notes..
....
....
....

❧ PIÑON FUDGE ❧

    1 (7-oz.) jar marshmallow creme
1-1/2 cups sugar
  2/3 cup evaporated milk
  1/4 cup butter
  1/4 teaspoon salt
    1 (12-oz.) pkg. semi-sweet chocolate chips
    1 cup piñon nuts
    1 teaspoon vanilla extract

1. In a heavy saucepan, combine marshmallow creme, sugar, evaporated milk, butter and salt. Bring to a full rolling boil over moderate heat, stirring constantly. Boil 5 minutes, stirring constantly.

2. Remove from heat. Add chocolate chips and stir until melted and smooth. Stir in piñon nuts and vanilla extract.

3. Pour into a foil-lined 8-inch-square pan. Chill until firm.

Makes about 2 lbs.

The Spanish language spoken here is a product of an interesting mix of Mexican, American Indian, Anglo and a dialect spoken in 16th-century Spain. This unique dialect is found only in New Mexico and linguists recognize it instantly.

Notes..
....
....
....

OTHER SOUTHWEST SPECIALTIES

Some of my favorite recipes don't fit neatly into the usual cookbook categories, as I found to my dismay while writing this cookbook. So I'm creating a special chapter for those I must share with you—what we might call "extras" but just can't leave out.

I'm including quite a variety, from salsas to egg dishes which make marvelous entrées for brunch. The beverages give you a special touch of the Southwest. The relishes, chutney and other side dishes can add zest to any meal.

❧ BAKED CHILE OMELETTE ☙

1/4 lb. bacon, finely diced
1 (6-oz.) can cream-style corn
1 (4-oz.) can chopped green chiles
1 teaspoon sugar
1/8 teaspoon garlic powder
3 tablespoons light cream
6 large eggs
Salt, to taste
1 cup grated Cheddar cheese

1. Preheat oven to 375F(190C). Butter an 8-inch baking dish; set aside.

2. Fry bacon crisp and drain off excess grease.

3. Mix bacon with corn, chiles, sugar and garlic powder. Spread evenly in prepared dish.

4. In a bowl, combine cream, eggs and salt to taste. Pour over the corn-chile mixture. Sprinkle cheese on top.

5. Place on center rack of preheated oven and bake 35 to 40 minutes, or until egg mixture is set.

Makes 6 servings.

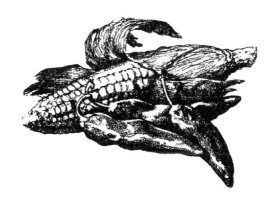

Notes ....
....
....
....

❧ SALSA POACHED EGGS ❧

1-1/2 cups fresh tomato salsa
  1/2 cup water
  12 large eggs
  12 corn or flour tortillas, warmed and crisped
   4 cups shredded lettuce

1. Place salsa and water in a large skillet.

2. Heat until mixture begins to bubble. Gently drop eggs into salsa without breaking the yolks.

3. Cover and poach over medium low heat; simmer, taking care not to allow liquid to boil.

4. Cook as desired.

5. Place on warm tortilla topped with lettuce and additional salsa.

Makes 6 servings.

Notes ....
....
....
....

⊷⟩ HUEVOS RANCHEROS ⟨⊶

---

2 cups Basic Green Sauce, page 128, or Basic Red Sauce,
    page 129
4 eggs
1/2 cup grated cheese

1. Heat chile sauce in a shallow skillet. When mixture begins to simmer, gently drop eggs into sauce without breaking the yolks.

2. Cover and poach over low heat, until eggs reach desired firmness.

3. Serve on warm plates with remaining sauce poured over eggs. Sprinkle with the grated cheese.

Makes 4 servings.

Some New Mexicans prefer to serve the poached eggs over softened corn tortillas, pouring additional sauce over them and garnishing with fresh tomatoes and grated Cheddar cheese.

Notes ....
....
....
....

❦ FIESTA HOT CHOCOLATE ❧

1/2 cup cocoa
1 tablespoon all-purpose flour
1/4 cup packed dark-brown sugar
4 cups milk
3 whole cloves
1 cinnamon stick, broken in half
2 tablespoons confectioners' sugar
1-1/2 teaspoons vanilla extract
Whipped cream
4 cinnamon sticks

1. Mix cocoa and flour in a 2-quart saucepan. Stir in brown sugar, milk, cloves and 1 cinnamon stick.

2. Heat to boiling over medium heat, stirring constantly; reduce heat. Simmer uncovered 5 minutes, DO NOT BOIL.

3. Remove from heat; remove cloves and cinnamon stick. Stir in confectioners' sugar and vanilla extract. Beat with wisk or hand beater until foamy. Pour into 4 cups or mugs.

4. Serve with whipped cream and a cinnamon stick in each mug.

Makes 4 servings.

Notes..
....
....
....

❧ CAFÉ MEXICANO ❧

8   cups water
1/3 cup packed dark-brown sugar
1/2 oz. baking chocolate, finely chopped
2   whole cloves
1   cinnamon stick, broken in half
1   cup regular grind coffee granules
1   teaspoon vanilla extract

1. In a 3-quart saucepan, heat water; add brown sugar, chocolate, cloves and cinnamon. Bring to a full boil, reduce heat and simmer uncovered 15 minutes. Stir in coffee. Remove from heat and let stand 5 minutes.

2. Stir in vanilla extract; strain through 4 thicknesses of cheesecloth or double thickness of coffee filters.

3. Pour coffee into cups and serve.

Makes 8 servings.

COFFEE DIABLO
1/4 cup brandy
8   teaspoons coffee liqueur
Whipped cream
Ground cinnamon

1. Prepare Café Mexicano as directed above. Return coffee to saucepan after straining. In a small, longhandled pan, heat brandy slightly. Remove from heat; ignite. Pour flaming brandy over coffee. Allow flame to burn out; stir.

2. Pour coffee in cups. Top each with whipped cream and one teaspoon of coffee liqueur. Garnish with a sprinkle of ground cinnamon.

Notes..
....
....
....

⊰{ HOT PICKLED }⊱ VEGETABLES

1/4	lb. whole green beans
1	cup thinly sliced carrots or 2 carrots, cut diagonally into thin slices
1	cup broccoli flowerets
3	celery stalks, cut into 2 x 1/4-inch strips
1-1/2	cups cauliflowerets
1	cup pearl onions
1/2	cup coarse salt
1/2	cup serrano or jalapeño chiles, canned or fresh
1/4	teaspoon ground cloves
2	cups cider vinegar
2	tablespoons black peppercorns
2	cups water

1. Combine all ingredients in a large glass or plastic container.

2. Cover and refrigerate at least 48 hours, but no longer than 2 weeks.

Makes 10 servings.

Notes..
....
....
....

❦{ JALAPEÑO JELLY }❦

1/2   cup chopped jalapeño peppers, seeded
3/4   cup chopped green bell peppers, seeded
  6   cups sugar
1-1/2 cups apple-cider vinegar
1/4   teaspoon butter
  1   6-oz. bottle liquid fruit pectin
       Green food coloring
       Paraffin, melted

1. Place all peppers in food processor or blender; grind fine using pulsing action.

2. Place peppers in a large pot; add sugar and vinegar. Bring to a full boil; continue hard-boil 1 minute. Mixture will swell to 3 times its initial volume. Add butter to control froth.

3. Remove from heat and allow to cool about 5 minutes. Add liquid fruit pectin and stir well. Add food coloring, 1 drop at a time, to achieve desired color.

4. Pour into hot sterilized half-pint jars and seal with paraffin.

Makes about 5 to 7 jars.

✚ **VARIATION**: Add 1/2 cup fresh or frozen raspberries or 1/4 cup diced orange peel. They add a zesty flavor to this unusual jelly.

Notes...
....
....
....

⊰{ BIG JIM CHUTNEY }⊱

---

  2 lbs. Big Jim or anaheim green chiles, roasted, peeled,
          seeded, deveined, diced
  2 cups sugar
  1 tablespoon roasted Mexican oregano
2/3 cup cider vinegar
  1 teaspoon salt

1. Combine all ingredients and cook in a non-stick skillet over medium heat 15 minutes.

2. Allow to cool and serve cold.

Makes 6 servings.

Each September, the town of Hatch celebrates with their famous Chile Festival. Visitors enjoy a parade, along with competitions for the biggest and hottest chile. Great spicy foods are highlighted at this event.

Notes...
....
....
....

❧ BLAZING PEPPER SALSA ❧
for home canning

---

7   cups (about 5 lbs.) peeled, cored, seeded, chopped
    tomatoes
4   cups chopped white onions
5   cups chopped jalapeño peppers, seeded
2   cups chopped serrano peppers, seeded
3   teaspoons salt
3/4 cup vinegar
1/8 teaspoon Cayenne pepper

1. Prepare home canning jars and lids according to manufacturer's instructions.

2. Combine all ingredients in a large pot. Heat to simmering. Simmer 10 minutes.

3. Carefully ladle hot salsa into hot jars, leaving 1/4-inch headspace. Wipe rim and threads of jar with clean damp cloth. Place lid on jar with sealing compound next to glass. Screw band down evenly and firmly. Do not use excessive force.

4. Process 15 minutes in water-bath canner.

Makes about 7 half-pints.

Notes..
....
....
....

❧ TRADITIONAL SALSA ❧
for home canning

---

  7 cups (about 5 lbs.) peeled, seeded, chopped tomatoes
  6 green onions, sliced
  2 jalapeño peppers, seeded, diced
  2 tablespoons minced fresh cilantro
  4 garlic cloves, minced
  2 teaspoons salt
  4 drops of hot pepper sauce
1/2 cup vinegar
  2 tablespoons lime juice

1. Prepare home canning jars and lids according to manufacturer's instructions.

2. Combine all ingredients in a large pot. Bring mixture to a boil. Reduce heat and simmer 10 minutes.

3. Carefully ladle hot salsa into hot jars, leaving 1/4-inch headspace. Wipe rim and threads of jar with clean damp cloth. Place lid on jar with sealing compound next to glass. Screw band down evenly and firmly. Do not use excessive force.

4. Process 15 minutes in water-bath canner.

Makes about 4 pints.

Notes ....
....
....
....

APPENDIX

FRESH\DRY CHILES IN SEASON AUGUST-MARCH

Pecos Valley Pepper Company
P. O. Box 6074
Roswell, NM 88202

*Price list available upon request.
UPS shipping.*

SOUTHWEST SPECIALTY ITEMS

Twenty-one Varieties of Beans
    and One Pea
Gallina Canyon Ranch
144 Camino Escondido
Santa Fe, NM 87501
505-982-4149, FAX 505-986-0936

*Product list available upon
request. Send $1.00 and SASE.*

Gourmet Chile Products
P.O. Box 30822
Albuquerque, NM 87190

CANDY-PECANS-PIÑON SPECIALTIES

Señor Murphy, Candymaker
1904 Chamisa Street
P. O. Box 2505
Santa Fe, NM 87504
505-988-4311

Price list available on request.

HOT PRODUCTS FROM CHILES

Magnum Enterprises
P. O. Box 546
Jamez Springs, NM 87025

SEED DISTRIBUTORS

D. V. Burrell Seed Growers Co.
Rocky Ford Seed House
Box 150
Rocky Ford, CO 81067
719-254-3318, FAX 719-254-3319

*Offers chile, onion and other
seeds not found in other
catalogs. Free catalog available
on request.*

Shepherd's Garden Seeds
30 Irene Street
Torrington, CT 06790
203-482-3638

also

6116 Highway #9
Felton, CA 95019
408-335-6910

Catalog on request, $1.00.

MAIL ORDER SPICES

Pecos Valley Pepper Company
P. O. Box 6074
Roswell, NM 88202

Price list available on request.

Southwest Saw Corporation
3015 Broadway
Houston, TX 77017
713-645-2436, FAX 713-645-5407

Free price list available on request.

MAGAZINE

Chile Pepper Magazine
P.O. Box 4278
Albuquerque, NM 87196
505-266-8322 or 800-959-5468

Published bi-monthly. Complete source of chile information. 6 issues $18.95.

NEWSLETTER

The Chile Institute
Box 30003, Dept 3Q
Las Cruces, NM 88003
505-646-5171

A non-profit organization devoted to the study of Capsicums. Membership, $25 per year, includes subscription to newsletter.

SPECIAL THANKS TO

La Nelle Witt, Ph.D.
Eastern New Mexico University

Merv & N. Arlene Casey
Cheryl Doede, Mickie Palmer,
Paul Davis, and Jim Martinez